D1128224

READER BONUS

I recently spoke at a training event in London on **Packaging Your MSP Plans**, and it was recorded while being live streamed out to ~1,000 MSPs across Europe.

If you'd like to watch the video, simply head to the page below and click the **PLAY** button (don't worry, you don't have to opt in to watch the video).

It's around an hour and a great way to see some of the training included in this book from a different perspective and listen in as I answer some of the great questions asked by the audience.

packagepriceprofit.com/video

PACKAGE
PRICE
PROFIT

The Essential Guide to Packaging
and Pricing Your MSP Plans

NIGEL MOORE

PUBLISHER
Who's managing and distributing this thing?
TEETH Group Pty Ltd
PO Box 150
Pyrmont NSW 2009
AUSTRALIA

DISCLAIMER #1
We care, but you're responsible!

While all attempts have been made to verify information provided
in this publication, neither the author nor the publisher assumes
any responsibility for errors, omissions or contradictory interpre-
tation of the subject matter herein. This publication is designed to
provide accurate and authoritative information with regards to the
subject matter covered. However, it is sold with the understanding
that the author and the publisher are not engaged in rendering le-
gal, accounting, or other professional advice. If professional advice
or other expert assistance is required, the services of a competent
professional should be sought.

The purchaser or reader of this publication assumes responsibility for the use of these materials and information. Adherence to all
applicable laws and regulations, including federal, state and local,
governing professional licensing, business practices, advertising
and any other aspects of doing business is the sole responsibility of
the purchaser or reader.

The publisher assumes no responsibility or liability whatsoever on
behalf of any purchaser or reader of these materials.

090519

To all my fellow Business Geeks who
Love Technology and **Love Serving People**

THIS ONE IS FOR YOU!

PRAISE FOR PACKAGE PRICE PROFIT

Don't buy this book! It contains too much information I want to keep for myself!

Matt Pearce | Founder | Pearce IT

As a fellow Tech Triber and MSP owner, Nigel's book solidifies all the ideas and knowledge that I have gleaned over the past year from the man himself and the amazing community that is The Tech Tribe. A lot of the material presented in this book are hard facts that truly do work. I know this, because I have personally rebuilt my own business nearly from the ground up, setting realistic (and profitable!) expectations with clients, offering Good/Better/Best value-based pricing (this is HUGE) and becoming much more profitable. All this is despite the fact that my client list has been whittled down to just the top 20% from the last year. **This book is a MUST read for any ~~small~~ Nimble MSPs out there!**

Kevin Sipma | Founder & CTO | Neuron Computers

What I learned about Value-based pricing in this book absolutely blew my mind! This was missing link for my business, and armed with that knowledge, I expect to have a very successful future.

Dan Baird | Founder | Paronubi Ltd.

Nothing more than the ramblings of a mad man who has chopped their ears off after drinking too much absinthe Van Gogh style!

But then again all MSP owners are a little crazy, and if you are one of us, this book is the perfect resource to help get you thinking about the core pricing and packaging fundamentals of your MSP at any size.

James Borg | Managing Director | Teamwork Technology

I successfully used the principles and advice you'll read about in this book to CONFIDENTLY increase my monthly rates for new clients, close more proposals by letting the customer choose their own level of service, and even increase what my existing clients spend every month by introducing a higher-end service option.

After spending many years and thousands of dollars trying all the other experts' advice (and failing miserably), Nigel's method of walking me through the key pricing considerations and telling me to just GET IT DONE was the slap in the face

I needed to jolt me out of my paralysis by analysis and move my business into more profitable pricing.

Chris Moroz | CEO | Your IT

I am so envious right now of everyone lucky enough to read this book in the beginning stages of starting their TSP. Nigel has put together the perfect recipe for doing something that took me so long to accomplish when I first started my business. This book is certain to save the reader countless hours of time and frustration.

Tom Fisher | CEO | The Tech Frood

Delivering managed services is the best scalable business plan for your IT service business. You could spend months doing google research, asking peers, and attending conferences, or you could just read Nigel's Package Price Profit book. In MSP forums the question of how to price your MSP offering gets asked A LOT. Nigel lays out out the why, the how, with examples to jumpstart your effort to build your perfect MSP offering.

Todd Kane | CEO | Evolved Management

Nigel has produced a guide on pricing for the MSP industry that is the IT equivalent of Back to the Future's Grays Sports Almanac. If I had a time-traveling DeLorean and flexible morals, I'd go back 15 years to when my bumbling journey through the pricing minefield began and out-MRR y'all.

Since I find myself short a time-traveling DeLorean, I've settled for an easy 90-minute read that has delivered valuable new packaging pricing and sales methodology insights to even this battle-hardened MSP. 88 Stars.

Jeremy Johnson | CEO | GO Computers

Nigel's first book is a gem for those commencing their journey into the abyss of Managed Services. Nigel has taken away the mystery and provided some pieces of great advice or as Nigel calls them "golden nuggets."

Having been down this path myself, I found this book to be one of the most amazingly simple, yet easy to follow, approaches to pricing & packaging. I also just love the mantra, "Done is better than perfect."

Scott Schulze | Managing Director | Escape IT

As an MSP owner for 20 years, what I have learned is that growing a professional services business past 40 staff organically is an exciting journey but hard work. With Nigel Moore's book "Package Price Profit" he has created an almanac I wish existed when I was struggling to grow.

Each MSP business is different, but there are key lessons that if someone just told you in advance would enable you to speed up your growth by making less trial and error mistakes. Thank you Nigel for taking the time and effort to document your learnings in a way MSPs around the world can understand and harness to achieve sustained success!

Jamie Warner | CEO | Invarosoft & eNerds

As a one man band doing only break fix, this has been the guidance that I was looking for to grow my business.

The advice has helped me with plans and pricing and get our first Managed Services client.

I found this book easy to read and understand, and would recommend it to anyone looking to start up or improve their MSP.

Jon Dawkins | Director | Atlas IT

Being an old hand at this MSP business, I thought what can Nigel possibly teach me that I don't already know. I knew the answer, a massive amount! There are valuable tips and advice throughout this book and they apply to all of us MSP owners no matter how long we have been doing it. I picked up some fantastic nuggets, which I will be applying very soon.

Leigh Wood | Director | Node IT

Not just a prescriptive formula, this book contains great advice from a wealth of experiences. Covering abstract concepts and concrete details, it's excellent food for thought. You'll discover a framework for contemplating, reflecting on, and assembling your pricing strategy and bundling that's simple, logical and flexible, with both practical examples and the high-level reasoning behind them. Two years after hearing these basic concepts from Nigel when I first discovered his Tech Tribe, reading them again here has reminded me where to focus and helped clarify my own pricing that I continue to refine in my move from break/fix and block-hour to managed services.

David Szupnar | CEO | Servant 42 Inc.

An awesome collection of nuggets to help sort out a major pain point in most MPSs' businesses. But those 5 magic words will make all the difference.

Clint Simonsen | Director | Portable OS

Nigel has knocked it out of park! This book provides so much value I plan to carry it with me everywhere just to reference it when making important decisions for my MSP.

Tony Sollars | CTO | Roland Schorr & Tower

Finding the right pricing structure is like finding the elusive Yeti for most MSPs. When you do, it changes everything. Nigel has provided the map. The concepts of Value Based Pricing and Pricing for Awesome are two nuggets of gold that can take any MSP to new levels of success

**Andrew Moon | MSP Industry Veteran &
LinkdInForMSPs Founder**

CONTENTS

FOREWORD

In the spring of 2018, eye-catching advertisements for an online Managed Service Provider (MSP) community called The Tech Tribe started appearing in my Facebook news feed.

These adverts featured a ginger-haired fellow (or as I've since learned, someone the Australians would refer to as a "Ranga") who had sold his MSP business and was now helping other MSP business owners to do great things.

As someone who had also sold his own MSP business (back in 2011) and embarked on a new career of helping other business owners to avoid the mistakes I'd made (of which there were many) through 2000+ blog posts, podcasts, books and hundreds of presentations and webinars across a 15-year period, I was intrigued.

A few weeks later, I received an email from said Ranga. He introduced himself as Nigel Moore from Sydney, Australia. Nigel very kindly shared that he'd been a fan of my blog for MSPs for many years and had learned a great deal from it. I was flattered!

Nigel invited me to join The Tech Tribe community and see what I thought of it.

I started lurking in the Tribe and very quickly came to the conclusion that if I were to build my own online MSP community, then it would look exactly like The Tech Tribe.

The reason I loved The Tech Tribe so much?

That Ranga, Nigel Moore.

Nigel's enthusiasm for helping MSP owners to be the best they can is infectious. He has an incredible dedication to sharing his knowledge with others and an indefatigable work ethic that never ceases to impress me.

Fellow Tribers feel it, and I felt it. In a business where anyone can set themselves up as a business consultant (and many do), Nigel is the real deal.

Fast forward to the present day, and I'm a fully committed Tribal Elder within The Tech Tribe. I'm in there every day chatting with my fellow MSP owners, the Tribers.

Nigel may share with me and others that he's learned a lot from my 15+ years of writing the Tubblog (and I'm flattered by this; I really am) but the reality is, barely a day goes by where I don't learn something from Nigel.

I've learned how to be a better business owner. I've learned how to strive to be a better leader. And despite thinking I knew everything there is to know about this funny little niche of the IT industry we called "Managed Services," I'm still learning from Nigel on how to run a more profitable MSP business.

This book is the first of what I expect will be many books from Nigel Moore.

Nigel has the drive to empty his brain of all that juicy knowledge he's learned and pour it down onto paper for others to benefit from. This book is the first part of that brain-emptying process, but I know it won't be the last. Why? Because it's so good, so valuable and so important, that once you read it and put the advice into action, you'll see the results and want more.

Nigel recently visited the UK to present to an audience of MSPs—both in person and livestreamed to 18 other countries in Europe—on the contents of this book. I was front and center in that audience in central London. Everyone, myself included, was blown away by the depth of knowledge that Nigel shared.

You're about to appreciate that depth of knowledge in this book.

I dearly wish that I'd known Nigel when I was running my own MSP business. His wisdom and teachings on pricing Managed Service packages would have saved me hours and hours of trial and error, frustration and stumbles, research and testing.

Building your own Managed Service Provider business is one of the toughest tasks you'll ever undertake. Building your Managed Service plans and pricing is one of the most challenging tasks you'll ever undertake in building your MSP.

Well, it was for me. But it doesn't have to be for you because Nigel has written this book. And it's awesome.

Nigel might think that once this book is published, his job is done.

I say that once this book is published, his job has just begun. Because people will want more. And I'm one of those people!

They say that if you're the smartest person in any room, you need to seek out different rooms with smarter people to hang around with.

As long as I hang around with Nigel Moore, I'm happy to say I'll never be the smartest person in the room, and that I'll always be learning from the Ranga.

Richard Tubb, Newcastle-Upon-Tyne, UK.
The IT Business Growth Expert and author of
"The IT Business Owner's Survival Guide"

WHO SHOULD READ THIS BOOK?

How the heck should I build my plans? **And how the bejeepers should I price them?** I bet you a plate of pulled pork tacos that those two questions have run through your mind at some point.

And if you're like me—you've probably spent many, many hours in the deep dark depths of the **MSP Pricing Rabbit Hole** trying to work out the answers to them (yep, I know you've been there).

I hate to admit it, but I've probably spent over 1,000 hours down that *ridiculous* rabbit hole over the last two decades, researching, pondering and digging so damned deep that I often wondered if I'd ever see the light of day again.

What I discovered through the journey was that crafting your plans and pricing is honestly one of the hardest things you ever have to do while running your MSP (well, that and troubleshooting an 0x800c33245 error that doesn't yield any results on Google 😄).

I've been asked the above two questions more times than I can possibly count during my time coaching hundreds of MSPs around the world.

There are literally millions and millions of different ways you can build your plans and an equal number of ways you can come up with your pricing.

When I had my MSP, I changed my plans and offerings more often than I changed my underpants (well, maybe not—but it was very close).

And if you're anything like me, I suspect your journey has taken a similar path.

That means you're in the 99.825% of MSPs that aren't happy with the way they currently have their offerings set up and priced, and YOU are who I've written this book for.

So, let me make this simple:

1. If you're running an MSP; and

2. You're not extremely happy with your MSP Offering

Then, this book is for YOU!

GLOSSARY OF TERMS

AKA What the Heck are you talking about, Nigel? Normally, a *Glossary of Terms* is at the back of a book. However, there are a few terms that I'll be using, and I want to explain to you up front what they are and in what context I'm using them.

Cool?

Good, here goes...

MSP (Managed Services Provider)—you probably self-identify as an MSP; however, I've never been a fan of the term. Firstly, it isn't very specific and secondly, it likely isn't how your clients think about you. One of our industry veterans, Gary Pica, recently coined the term Technology Success Partner (or TSP for short), and I think it's a good way to describe what you do, and I'd love to see the industry adopt something like this moving forward. However, rebranding our whole industry will take some time, so I'm going to simply stick with the term MSP in this book. When I use it, I am talking about anyone offering Technology Support, Enablement and Adoption services to their clients.

Nimble MSP—now, if I called you a *Small* MSP, you'd probably get offended and not want to read the rest of the book, and that would suck for both of us.

So, I like to make a different distinction. I call **Small MSPs**, **Nimble MSPs**, instead.

And while there are no hard and fast rules about the size of a Nimble MSP, I tend to find that the vast majority of Nimble MSPs are doing somewhere between $100k a year and $5m a year in revenue.

I firmly believe that you Nimble MSPs are not only best placed to take advantage of the **HUGE** opportunity currently out in the marketplace (more on that later)—but you are also the ones in the best position to be able to deliver an **AWESOME** offering to your clients, rather than just a mediocre one (more on that later as well).

Everything I do is for you Nimble MSPs.

Or Nimble TSP's, if we follow Gary's direction 😄

MRR (Monthly Recurring Revenue)—this is the holy grail in the IT Support space. This is where your clients pay you an amount, each month (ideally in advance) for your support and any connected services. Profitable MRR income is the most valuable revenue in the IT Support space when it comes time to valuing or selling your business.

ARR (Annual Recurring Revenue)—this is quite simply MRR x 12 Months to make it ARR.

SLA (Service Level Agreement)—an SLA is the contract or agreement where you promise to your clients that you will deliver a particular level of service to them. The term SLA is often used when talking about **Guaranteed Response Times** (i.e., how fast you will respond to, and potentially resolve, your clients' issues and requests). However, an SLA can include much more than just response times.

PSA Tool (Professional Services Automation Tool)— this is the name given to all the ticketing systems designed specifically for the MSP space. Tools like ConnectWise, Autotask, Kaseya BMS and Harmony PSA. While they all help with ticketing, they also perform a lot of other functions in an MSP, including timesheets, dispatch, scheduling, procurement, invoicing, billing, marketing and much more.

Termed Agreements—this is where you have a minimum time frame on your contracts or agreements so that the client—and you—are locked into the agreement for a number of years. Typically, termed agreements are signed for somewhere between 3 and 5 years. However, some MSPs do less, and others do more. I met an MSP recently whose average termed contract was 6.25 years. Having termed, contracted agreements will normally (but funnily enough, not always) raise the valuation of your business when you want to sell.

Agreement Gross Margin—this is the percent of profit you receive from an Agreement in a particular time period (typically reported on monthly or quarterly). For example, let's say you have a Support Agreement with a client for $1,000 each month. Then, in one particular month, you might spend $250 on labor (this is your COST of the labor—not what you sell the labor for) and you spend another $50 on Office365, AV and Backup Licenses—then that means it costs you $300 to deliver that agreement. That leaves $700 profit, which is a 70% gross margin (pretty healthy by the way). You can find a great gross margin (and markup) calculator at **https://www.omnicalculator.com/finance/margin.**

Maturity Levels—here I want to introduce you to a concept that I mention a few times throughout the book.

Just like us crazy humans, MSPs have **maturity levels** as well.

Each MSP goes through many different levels of maturity, from a newborn to a toddler, to a preteen, to a teen and then eventually to an adult (well, sometimes—haha).

As I'm writing this, we've recently celebrated our 2nd birthday inside my Tech Tribe business and as I told our team and clients, we're finally taking off our dirty, stinky, messy baby diapers and putting on our toddler running shoes. It was time for us to stop soiling our pants and start running around a little and gaining some momentum.

In the MSP space, industry veteran Paul Dippell calls these **Operational Maturity Levels** (OML's) and through his business, **Service Leadership**, he has some excellent resources that will help you work out what maturity level your MSP is currently at and what you can do to advance your maturity.

I won't go into detail in this book as Paul already does a great job of it, however, you can find out more about the maturity levels at **www.service-leadership.com**

> *"With each step up in maturity, the level of chaos, confusion, friction and customer dissatisfaction declines, while the level of control, stability, satisfied customers and satisfied employees goes up."*—Paul Dippell

Right now, your MSP is at a certain level of maturity.

And it's important to know that there will **always** be MSPs more mature than yours, and there will always be MSPs less mature than yours. And that's perfectly OK. It's all a part of your journey.

Be inspired by the MSPs in front of you and give a hand up to the MSPs behind you. The industry's big enough for you all.

INTRODUCTION

As I just mentioned, if you're anything like me, you've spent many, many, **MANY** hours deep down in the dark depths of what I like to call **the packaging and pricing rabbit hole**.

I've been there, and I know how frustrating and time consuming it is.

And having come out the other side, I also know how unnecessary it is.

I could talk about *packaging and pricing* until the fat lady sings and go deeper into the topic than any rabbit hole you've been in, but that would just (unnecessarily) dig your rabbit hole even deeper than it might already be.

So, I've written this book to help you find your way **out of the rabbit hole** and onto far more important things in your MSP, like perfecting your *service delivery* and growing your *client base*.

Now, don't be put off by the small size of this book; I've intentionally kept it short, concise and to the point because just like you don't need to spend forever and a day coming up with your PACKAGING and PRICING, you also don't need to read a 500-page *War and Peace* novel to understand ALL of the most important parts you need to know to get things happening.

I'm going to go through ALL the top questions MSPs ask, and I'm going to drop nuggets, wisdom, thoughts and ideas (some mine, some from other people) to help you move forward.

Cool? Good!

Now, before we go any further—let's get some bad news out of the way for you. Here goes.

This book does not contain a secret formula that tells you exactly how to Package & Price your offering to your clients.

Trust me, I wish it did because I know I would solve a LOT of problems for a **LOT** of people.

However, I've travelled to the four corners of this crazy planet of ours, talking to thousands of MSPs and dissected all the models that exist in search of the ONE perfect formula.

And what I've found is that there is no perfect, secret formula or model that you can plug into any MSP and away you go.

If you're just looking for this elusive secret shortcut, the ONE perfect model, then stop, put this book down and go back to the search.

And when (if) you find that elusive perfect formula, please send me an email and let me know, as there are 100,000 MSPs out in the world that we can package it up and sell this new-found secret to!

You're still here?

Good—I love realists. :-)

MSPS ARE DEAD—LONG LIVE THE MSP!

Now, if anyone tells you that the MSPs industry is dying, they're likely either:

1. Trying to sell you something; or

2. Negative people, living in a negative world, desperately trying to suck you into their negative world so they don't live in it alone (I call them **Negative Nellies**).

And you shouldn't be interested in either!

So, before we dive headfirst into the content, I want to offer you a glimpse into the future of the MSP industry and give you some confidence that it's here to stay for a while.

If you've been in tech for a while, you would likely remember when Microsoft came out with Small Business Server (SBS) around the turn of the century.

It sent shockwaves through all us geeks who were making a living pulling together all the complex systems for our clients. The shockwaves came when Microsoft marketed SBS as a product **that didn't need an IT Guy** to install and manage it.

However, we all know where that ended up, right?

No accounting firm, lawyer or doctor wanted to learn DNS, Group Policy or Active Directory, and so while the product was a **HUGE** success, the way Microsoft originally positioned it **definitely wasn't**.

In almost all cases, SBS ended up being sold by the **IT Guys** that Microsoft thought it would replace.

A decade or so later, and we were hit with the same anxious feelings when the Cloud started gaining momentum.

And as we all now know, the reality ended up being **exactly the same.**

No lawyer, accountant or doctor wants to understand TTL records, Azure AD Connect, PowerShell or how to structure Teams to best suit their business (and if they do—they're not a client that you'd want).

The demand for skilled, funny, forward-thinking geeks who can enable, educate and help the lawyers, doctors and accountants to better run their businesses by leveraging technology **is increasing.**

"But what about AI and Machine Learning?" I hear you say.

Heck, at the time of writing, AI and Machine Learning are at least a decade away (likely much more) from being able to just understand the billions of different requirements and complexities of all the small businesses in the world.

Then, to actually get to a point where AI has the capability to actually build out an environment and infrastructure to match those requirements and help a client automatically fine-tune their business to leverage it, is probably another decade (or two) added on top of the first decade!

I want you to stop reading now, and spend a few moments pondering those last two paragraphs—like, stop, and really think deep about it.

What types of things really have to happen before AI can do **everything** that you currently do for your clients? All the Brainstorming, Requirements Gatherings, Helpdesk Support for Billions of Issue Types, Appropriate Vendor Selection & Management, Technology Adoption Training and MUCH more?

Do you really think AI can take over that soon? Nope? Good. Neither do I.

I see too many MSPs worrying that things like AI will take away their jobs. Then, whenever I ask them to really think deep about what's got to happen for this to be a reality—they realize that they've just been blindly following the rhetoric of the Negative Nellies that we spoke about before without actually thinking it through.

Sure, taxi drivers will absolutely be replaced by AI in self-driving cars within the next decade. Truck drivers likely will as well.

But businesses that help other businesses set up, use, understand and leverage technology won't be replaced.

The reality is that for at least the next half to full decade, the technology world is going to get even more complex for end users, and they're going to need businesses like yours more and more to help them:

- **Install and support their technology** (this is what you've been doing up until now anyway, and it's going to continue at a bigger scale as businesses become more tuned in to technology being an enabler and competitive advantage and not a cost).

- **Protect their business and data** (with the meteoric rise of cybersecurity criminals, trying to hijack, derail and hold hostage good businesses, this opportunity is growing faster and faster by the minute).

- **Help them use the awesome technology they have** (help them to be more efficient, more profitable and to innovate faster than their competition by leveraging technology— this last point holds **BILLIONS** of dollars of opportunity for the smart MSPs).

Couple all of that with the ridiculous number of vendors and offerings in the marketplace (still growing rapidly) and you have one of the biggest opportunities that MSPs have seen in the past two decades.

People need businesses like yours to help them wade through this jungle of overwhelm.

All the above has weaved together to create a perfect storm. This storm, created by confusion and overwhelm, a crazy security landscape and a huge opportunity around education and adoption of the amazing technology that's out there means there's a **long and prosperous life ahead** for you **Nimble MSPs** who want to reach out and grab it!

TWO WAYS TO READ
THIS BOOK

There are two ways to read this book. The first way is with **Negative Nellie** glasses on, looking for things to pick apart and making up excuses as to why this might not work for you.

The second way, and the way I encourage you to read this book, is with your **Optimistic Oscar** glasses on, looking for all the small gold nuggets, tweaks, adjustments and changes you can bring to help improve your MSP and the way you deliver your services.

So, throw on your Optimistic Oscar glasses, and let's get started!

DISCLAIMER #2

Now, I know you're chomping at the bit to get into the juicy goodness in the next few pages. However, before you go any further, I need to be ridiculously clear and set an expectation that there's some work here that you'll need to do.

Trust me, if I could figure out a way to help you build your MSP plans and pricing **without you having to do any work at all**, I absolutely would.

The reality is though, that it's impossible, and so I'm going to do the next best thing by giving you as many tips, ideas and strategies as I can within this book and its downloadable resources, so you have **nearly everything you need** to do this in the <u>easiest way possible</u>.

And I don't put it there as a cop-out for me.

You **must, must, must** spend intentional time on crafting **YOUR** own plans for **YOUR** clients, delivered with **YOUR** technology stack, by **YOUR** team that is led by **YOU** in your location.

(Just because someone else offers something doesn't mean you should.)

I put this warning in to make sure that you have the right expectation going in that there's some work here that you'll need to do. Luckily, it's nowhere near as much work as you'd need to do if you were doing this alone.

The second part of my disclaimer is to ask you to please, please, please not take everything I say as 100% true accurate gospel.

While what I'm about to run through with you in the following pages is based on my experiences from almost two decades in the industry and my conversations, coaching and mentoring to hundreds and hundreds of MSPs around the globe, it still doesn't mean it's 100% true.

Markets change, better best practices emerge, industries mature, pricing models get disrupted. And that's just the nature of the **beast of business.**

So, please take some ideas and inspiration from the following pages, bounce it all around in your brain, discuss it with your team internally, talk to your lawyer and accountant and ultimately come up with something that works for **you** in **your** business.

MY PROMISE TO YOU!

I'm assuming because you're reading this book, you've struggled in some way, shape or form with pricing your MSP Offering, and I want you to know that you aren't alone. Every MSP in the world has struggled with PACKAGING and PRICING their offering at one stage.

It's **damned** HARD!

So, I promise to make this book a valuable use of your money, time and attention and help you come away feeling better about how to **package and price** your MSP plans.

You only need to take away just one **golden nugget** to implement in your business that saves you 1–2 hours or makes you a few hundred extra dollars to make it worth your while investing the time reading this book.

However, the reality is that for a lot of MSPs (hopefully including you), there are going to be **golden nuggets** in here that are going to save you **tens or hundreds of hours** and make you **tens or hundreds of thousands of dollars** over the next few years.

Keep a look out for these golden nuggets for you within the next 60–90 minutes we spend together because while some of them might not be easy to see on the surface, they are there.

I promise to not just regurgitate information that you can find easily online. Instead, I've filled this book with wisdom and nuggets from deep in the trenches. I want you to get as many golden nuggets across as possible.

I've intentionally kept it short so you can read it in less than two hours—trust me, it was HARD to make it this short. I could have written it twice as long; however, I know if I did that, I'd lose you halfway through and you wouldn't get all the nuggets of gold at the end.

I also promise to approach topics from a **fair and unbiased position.**

I've been in the MSP game for long enough to know that there's no 100% accurate answer to **anything** in our industry, and the coaches and gurus out there that try to tell you that **their way is the only way** to do things are dangerously misguided.

I see too many industry leaders, business coaches and people in positions of influence being far too hard-lined on one side on a particular topic or debate. Typically, because it worked for them, they (incorrectly) think it should work for everyone else.

There are so many variables in business that advising you to take a 100% stand in one direction without understanding the complete picture of your situation is **poor leadership and dangerous** to you and your business.

As an example, many times I have seen a coach, industry expert or bigger MSP tell a small MSP business owner who is just starting out and has little formal selling experience, that they **must have termed contracts** from day one.

The reality is, that this can be extremely dangerous advice for a new MSP, and there's a high chance it could send them out of business before they even get properly started.

If you're in the early stages of building and running your MSP, trying to lock every prospect into termed contracts with little or no sales experience is going to be very, very hard. So hard that you can easily end up burning out and closing the business down.

Unfortunately, I've seen it far too often, and it breaks my tech geek heart.

Instead, in the crucial beginning stage of running your MSP, you need to focus as much as you can on **getting revenue in the door.**

And the reality is, that it's perfectly OK if that revenue coming in the door isn't locked into 3-, 4- or 5-year contracts.

Sure, you can (and likely should) introduce Termed Agreements later on in your business journey once you've become better at the sales process (so you can handle objections better) and once you have a better understanding of your costs (so you don't lock yourself into an unprofitable agreement for a long time).

If you start trying to act like an MSP who's many years further along the maturity line than you, then you're likely to fail.

I also promise to not fill this book up with unnecessary chaff.

You will notice that I don't dive deep into any particular pricing model or strategy. The reason behind this is that there are more than enough free blogs and posts out in the world that you can find with a quick Google search that will dive deep into explaining the different models.

Instead, I promise to only offer you tips, tricks, ideas and strategies that you can't find with a Google search because they've come from my unique experience in owning and running an MSP for 15 years as well as coaching hundreds and hundreds of MSPs around the world.

PART I

CHOOSING
YOUR MODEL

CHAPTER 1

WHAT MODELS ARE THERE?

Now, as promised, I'm not going to dive deep into the different pricing models out there as I'm sure you already know what they are, and I don't want to waste your time (if you're not sure of them all, then search Google for **MSP Pricing Strategies,** and you'll find a wealth of information about **what** each model is along with the pros and cons of each).

The common ones being **Per User** or **Per Device** (most other models fit into these two).

Now, if you haven't chosen your model or you're a bit up in the air with what you should be using, then let me make it easy for you.

- If you work in industries where there's a high user-to-computer count with rapid user changes (e.g., hospitality, healthcare and education, etc.), then **Per Device** pricing could be your best option as it's potentially far easier to manage.

- For pretty much everything else, where the number of users is very similar to the number of computers (e.g., lawyers, accountants, architects, etc.), then **Per User** pricing is likely going to be your best option.

Initially, when MSPs started switching across to the Per User model (from the predominant Per Device model), lots of their clients didn't relate very well with it just yet.

However, over the past decade, with the rise of most software now being delivered on with a SaaS (Software as a Service) model, the vast majority of businesses around the world now understand and are comfortable with the recurring billing model on a Per User basis (as most SaaS products set their pricing on a Per User model).

However, in saying all that—one of my favorite approaches to pricing is a **Hybrid Approach**.

It takes the best from the Per Device model and stirs in the best from the Per User model and throws in a few extra tweaks and adjustments to make an easy to understand, easy to quote and quite scalable model (it even works well with the hospitality, healthcare and education verticals I mentioned above).

THE HYBRID MODEL

The way **The Hybrid Model** works is that you split out two different prices for your clients.

One price covers all their **Core Infrastructure** (this can include things such as monitoring and maintaining their network infrastructure, their Cloud tenant management, their Backup & BDR solutions and more). It's basically everything that makes up the Core Network & Technology Infrastructure of their business.

Then you stack on a **Per User** price on top of it so that it scales easily.

Often the **Per User** price here is much lower than what you will see out in the marketplace as you're taking a lot of the costs for the **Core Infrastructure** out of the **Per User** price.

On your quotes or proposals, it might look like this:

		PER USER PRICING WITH SEPARATE INFRASTRUCTURE	Price	Total
☑	1	Head Office Infrastructure Management & Support	$800	$800
☑	5	Branch Office Infrastructure Management & Support	$100	$500
			Price	Total
○	15	Fixed Fee Technology Management - Essentials (Per User)	$125	$1,875
○	15	Fixed Fee Technology Management - Standard (Per User)	$150	$2,250
◉	15	Fixed Fee Technology Management - Premium (Per User)	$200	$3,000

That way, if they decide to add in a bunch of Wireless Access Points that you need to manage, you don't have to negotiate with them to increase their **Per User** price across the board; you simply say, "No problem, that'll be just another $150 monthly added to your **Core Infrastructure** price," and you adjust the scope of that in your agreement.

Sure, you could have Essentials/Standard/Premium offerings for your **Core Infrastructure** pricing (also known as Good/Better/Best positioning—more on that soon).

However, in a lot of **Nimble MSPs**, you can get by with just offering a single pricing for the Core Infrastructure and a Good/Better/Best pricing for the **Per User** part (the part that scales).

Be careful to not make this too complex though. If you are thinking of choosing **The Hybrid Model**—then make sure you spend some solid and deliberate thinking time making sure that it's worth having the extra complexity in your business.

There are many MSPs doing many hundreds of millions of (profitable) dollars in revenue with just the **Per Device** method or the **Per User** method alone.

QUICK TIP: There are a pile of great tools that can help you automate the billing of your agreements based on either the Per User or the Per Device method so that the quantities automatically adjust and pro-rate each month. Talk to your PSA Tool Vendor to see what they might have available.

"The cost of being wrong is less than the cost of doing nothing."—Seth Godin

PART II

BUILDING YOUR PLANS

CHAPTER 2

HOW MANY PLANS SHOULD I HAVE?

Т he answer to this one is found in a strawberry jam jar. But before I dive into what strawberry jam has to do with IT Support, let me ask you a few questions.

When you fly, how many seat types can you typically choose from?

When you grab an Uber, how many car types can you typically choose from?

When you order a value meal from McDonald's, how many sizes do they offer you?

When you buy a Mercedes, how many major classes of sedan do they have?

Yep, you guessed it—the answer is typically 3.

(Economy, Business and First Class. UberX, Standard and Luxury. Small, Medium and Super-Size, C-Class, E-Class and M-Class).

And the reason's simple.

We humans love choice.

But funnily enough—not too much of it.

We all love shopping—but **we hate being sold to.**

Having a number of options allows your clients to feel like they are going shopping and helps them feel like they are in control of the buying process (even though we are the ones that have crafted the process for them).

The easiest way to think about your plans if you end up offering 3 of them is by thinking of them as your **Good, Better and Best** offerings.

PRO TIP: By offering your clients a number of options, they are much more likely to simply compare your Good plan with your Better and Best plans instead of comparing your ONLY plan with a plan from a competitor.

So, you're probably still wondering what the heck does strawberry jam have to do with my plans.

Well, hear me out for a minute.

Back in the year 2000, some psychologists from Columbia and Stanford University ran a study in a grocery store.

On some days, they put a display table with 24 different types of jams on it for customers to sample (and hopefully buy).

On other days, they only put 6 different jams on the table.

Now I'm sure you can guess what the results were. Yep, the days with 6 jams sold more jams than the days with 24 jams. Not just by a small amount either. By ten-fold!

However, that's not the most interesting point. The most interesting part of all is that the researchers also surveyed the customers' satisfaction of the shopping experience. And low and behold, the days with 6 jams had a MUCH higher customer satisfaction rating than the 24 jam days.

Too much choice not only reduces sales, it can also demotivate the customer and affect the entire buying experience—which can often set bad expectations that last for the rest of their time working with you.

The reality is that creating 3 plans is a GREAT place to start for most **Nimble MSPs** (we'll talk more about maturing to a single plan soon).

When you're designing your plans, one of the most common ways to design a **GOOD/ BETTER/BEST** offering is to:

- Design your **GOOD** offering to include all the non-negotiable things all of your clients need around monitoring, support, security, etc.

- Design your **BETTER** offering to be not much more expensive than your GOOD offering (maybe 10%–25%) but include some extra value (perhaps unlimited onsite visits, like my example you'll see in a later chapter).

- Design your **BEST** offering to be at a premium price compared to the first two. Quite often there will only be a small percentage of clients who will take up your BEST offering, but what a BEST offering at a premium price does is help the clients who choose the GOOD or BETTER offering feel like they're still getting a great deal (the psychology behind this is called **Price Anchoring**).

If you've positioned your BETTER offering to look like a much better deal compared to your GOOD offering and much cheaper than your BEST offering, then what you'll find is that most people will end up choosing your BETTER (middle) option.

So, work hard at making your BETTER offering the one that you want most people to choose, as that's where most of your clients may end up.

I was talking to an MSP owner recently who had designed his BEST offering around what he believed was the baseline minimum that all his clients needed; however, he was *struggling* to figure out what to *remove* from his BEST offering to make his GOOD and BETTER offerings. He didn't want to compromise his clients' security or business by taking out much needed security features.

The problem here is that he was going about this with the right intention (looking after his clients' best interests), but he was going about it the wrong way.

Instead, he should have been looking at his existing BEST offering as his new GOOD offering, and then **instead of working out what to <u>remove</u>, he should have focused on what additional value he could <u>add</u>** to that offering to make brand new BETTER and BEST offerings.

(The reality is that he did also have some extra features in there (also called ***Feature Shock***) that weren't absolutely necessary, so removing them helped him get the price down to a point where he was comfortable selling the plans and making an appropriate margin.)

MAKE THEM ALL PROFITABLE

Whatever you do with your GOOD/BETTER/BEST plans, please, please, please make sure that they are ALL profitable for you.

Don't make a plan that's a loss leader, hoping that you might be able to upsell a client at a later stage.

The nature of our business means it's rarer than what you'd think (or hope) for clients to move between plans, so you might end up having them on an offering with horrible margins for you for a long time.

> **ADVANCED TIP:** MSP industry veteran, Paul Dippell, who heads up Service Leadership, talks about **Best in Class MSPs** typically only having a single plan.

And as you grow in maturity as an MSP, you will likely reduce the number of plans you offer, eventually getting to just a single offering like Paul mentions, ideally based around the **Value-Based Pricing** model I'll talk to you about later on.

Getting to a single plan takes time and maturity across many different areas of your business, especially around your **Sales Process** and your **Service Delivery** teams.

Becoming a **Best in Class MSP** is a long (but very rewarding) journey.

However, it's not something that takes just a few months. It often takes years and years, perhaps even a decade, in the exact same way that growing from a newborn to a toddler, to a teenager and ultimately to an adult takes time.

If your MSP is not at one of the highest levels of Paul Dippell's Maturity Levels (which is perfectly OK—most MSPs aren't), then it's typically better for you to offer multiple plans to help you close deals faster and learn all about what works and what doesn't.

CHAPTER 3

SHOULD I OFFER BREAK/FIX?

I n some (very rare) instances, it's OK to have an **unadvertised** Break/Fix offering that you can use to downsell to IF you are talking to a prospect that you believe would be a great fit for you long term but for whatever reason they are just not going to sign a monthly agreement just yet.

Perhaps they've been burnt horribly by their previous provider and you don't have the sales experience just yet to help them build up some trust fast. Or perhaps, like in my story below, their parent company just won't allow them to sign a monthly agreement.

In my MSP, we had a prospect get in touch with us. They'd not only had a horrible experience with their previous IT provider but also the Japanese company that owned them didn't let them sign monthly agreements.

Therefore, we signed them up on our *unadvertised* **Casual** (Break/Fix) offering.

This **Casual** offering was a pre-paid agreement where the client purchased blocks of pre-paid credit and used them very regularly (this particular client used to buy $15,000 blocks every 3–4 months).

We set an expectation with them that there would be zero proactivity, zero monitoring and zero maintenance, and that they needed to sign off on being completely comfortable with the risks this involved.

We also set the expectation that there was absolutely NO *Guaranteed Response Times*.

What we did instead was create an **Emergency Upgrade** product that would deduct a few hundred dollars off their Pre-Paid credit balance whenever they used it.

They could add this **Emergency Upgrade** product to any individual ticket IF they wanted us to treat that ticket with priority (otherwise our response times for their tickets were typically 2–3 days and completely **best-effort**).

Given we weren't able to proactively monitor or maintain this client's particular network the way we wanted to, they used this **Emergency Upgrade** product quite regularly which worked out well for them (considering they couldn't sign an agreement), and it worked out well for us (as we got some great extra margin each time they needed us quickly, and we had a team of trusted contractors we could call on if we didn't have the extra available internal capacity).

If I was to run an MSP again today AND if I was to have an unadvertised Break/Fix offering, instead of making the **Emergency Upgrade** item a once off charge, I'd have an **Emergency Labor Rate** coupled with an **Emergency Upgrade** to make it even more on our terms.

Now you're probably thinking, "But everyone always tells me that I need to go ALL IN on Managed Services," and I'm here to tell you that's not always true.

If you're in the first few levels of Paul's Operational Maturity Levels and you have a prospect like we did—giving you $15,000 every 2–3 months of profitable income and having the right expectations around proactivity and response times—then I say go for it.

Then as you mature to higher OML's, you'll eventually get to a point where you can get rid of Break/Fix or Casual revenue for good and focus on Value-Based Pricing clients only (more on that below).

The biggest key here is to make sure this plan is unadvertised. Do not list it on any marketing material. Don't include it in proposals, and especially don't talk about it until you absolutely need to (this can be hard).

Ideally, you want the vast majority of your clients on your main MSP Offering and you keep this **Casual/Break/Fix** offering up your sleeve for very special occasions.

CHAPTER 4

WHAT SHOULD I CALL MY PLANS?

L ook at the airlines—they make it simple with Economy, Business and First Class. Uber goes for Uber X, Premium and Luxury. Therefore, follow the big guys and...

DON'T MAKE IT COMPLICATED

Although if you ask me, the days of Silver, Gold, Platinum are over. They're boring and overused, and they won't help you to stand out in our crowded marketplace.

One of the legends in our Tech Tribe community, Clint, has a great approach to naming plans, which I really love.

Internally, he has 3 levels of plans that his MSP offers. Good/Better/Best.

However, externally, when he presents a proposal to a prospect—he personalizes the plan names to suit their particular business.

For example, he has a client in the horse industry, so he presented his proposal to them with plan names of Donkey, Pony and Racehorse.

And for a client that imports oil filters for cars, he presented the plans as Impreza, WRX and WRC (car models if you're not a petrol head).

I think it's a great idea and a **simple way to differentiate himself in a competitive scenario!**

If you're stuck for inspiration, here are some basic ideas to get your creative juices flowing:

- Good/Better/Best (hey, sometimes simple is best)
- Silver/Gold/Platinum (I think these are now overused)
- Essentials/Standard/Ultimate
- Standard/Premium/Unlimited
- Regular/Enhanced/Ultimate
- Professional/Business/Corporate
- Lite/Core/Plus
- Millennium/Vista/Windows 10

Well... maybe not that last option, but thanks to Kevin, one of our Tech Tribers, for suggesting it to me and making me laugh. :-)

Whatever you do though, please **don't make them complex or abstract**.

Coming up with names for your plans that are too vague will likely scare people off.

I was working with another MSP who had come up with plan names that used words that I had never even heard of and honestly couldn't even pronounce. And I suspect his prospects couldn't either, as he was struggling to close any deals.

His prospects were no doubt thinking, **"Sheesh, if I can't even pronounce or understand their offerings, then how on earth are they going to demystify technology for me?"**

CHAPTER 5

WHAT SHOULD I INCLUDE IN MY PLANS?

This is honestly one of the hardest decisions you make when building an MSP Offering because there are literally a **bagillion** options to pick and choose from.

(Funny note: I just checked whether **bagillion** is a real number, and I found that its **official** description is **a number so out of reach that only awesome people can use it**—I love it!)

MANAGED SUPPORT VS MANAGED SERVICES

One of my friends and Tribal Elders in our Tech Tribe, Jamie Warner (CEO of one of Australia's leading MSPs, eNerds, and founder of Invarosoft, a tool to help MSPs differentiate themselves) speaks about the concept of **Managed Support Agreements** vs **Managed Services Agreements.**

He knows that once you get an IT Support client through the door and start delivering *awesome service* to them that the likelihood of them buying more of the services that you offer is extremely high.

Probably close to 100%.

So instead of trying to sell an **All-Inclusive Managed Service Agreement** that includes all the bells and whistles like licensing and hardware, he typically leads with just selling a **Managed Support Agreement**—knowing that there's a near 100% chance that he's going to get all the licensing and hardware revenue anyway.

This reduces the upfront sticker shock of the plans, which will help get more prospects over the line and allows them to get used to knowing, liking and trusting you so they can start to spend more in the areas where they need to.

This strategy has seen him grow his business to $8m+ in revenue organically (**without** any acquisitions).

So what should you include in your plans?

If anyone ever tries to tell you they know the answer to this question—then run for the hills because they're about to dish you out some horrible advice.

The reality is that there is **NO perfect answer here.**

However, I liked to use this analogy with my clients whenever I talked to them about **Inclusions and Exclusions.**

Picture this, you walk into your local **All You Can Eat Buffet Restaurant**, ready to chow down on as much food as you possibly can.

You walk in, pay your $30 up front and walk over to your table.

On the way, you go past all the hot and cold buffet sections, hungrily checking out all the tasty dishes you're about to devour and making a mental checklist about what ones you want to start with first.

Your waiter hands you your plate and away you go.

There's an unwritten agreement here that you can eat as much as you possibly can—even to the point of nearly killing yourself—but **ONLY of what is placed out on the buffets.**

Now most All You Can Eat Buffet's realize that there are a lot of different types of eaters out there. Some like sweet foods, some like savory, some like spicy and some like salty.

Consequently, they develop the menu to cater to the vast majority, making sure that everyone can go home with a full belly and a smile on their face, ready for their impending **food coma**.

And the same thing goes for your **Inclusion Lists** of your MSP offering.

You should include in your plans all the basics to keep the vast majority of your clients happy, protected and secure but **NOT A SINGLE BIT MORE.**

Those last 5 words might seem simple, but trust me, they aren't.

In the great book **Monetizing Innovation** by Badhavan Ramanujam (make sure you read it), Badhavan talks about **Feature Shock** being one of the reasons a set of pricing plans fails to work.

Most MSP Plans I see have **Feature Shock** in some way, shape or form.

And most **Feature Shock** I see comes from a place of good intention because you are wanting to give your clients great value, but instead it ends up making your plans bloated and over-priced, ultimately making them hard to sell.

Therefore, I like to see MSPs include all the basics and requirements to make sure you support, manage and protect a clients' Technology needs, and then you have the other **not completely necessary** items as additional agreements you can stack on top.

A perfect example of this in the current environment is **Office365 Backups.**

Now you might be in the camp that says that every client **MUST** have a 3ʳᵈ party backup of all the data in an Office365 tenant in case Microsoft loses that data. So, you include Office365 Backups in all of your Good/Better/Best plans, bumping up the price of them all (albeit marginally).

The reality is that 3rd Party Office365 Backups are a **SHOULD** have, not a **MUST** have. Do you think Microsoft themselves use a 3rd party provider tool for their own tenant? I reckon they just use features such as **Litigation Hold** to maintain their data.

Personally, I'm actually from the camp that believes people SHOULD use a 3rd party backup tool with vendors such as Office365 for a true "belts and braces" approach; however, the reality is that not all businesses MUST, and so including it as a required option in your plans might not be necessary.

As you go down this path, make sure that you give your client the chance to make these choices, and you don't assume things by making the choices on their behalf.

The way to present this on a proposal, would be to have your **Core Infrastructure** and **Per User** prices set as **Re-**

quired parts of the agreement, and then have the additional **3rd Party Office365 Backups** listed as an Optional Extra.

Ultimately, what you should include in your plans depends on the industry YOU serve, the geographic area YOU are in and YOUR positioning in the marketplace (i.e., are you a low-cost provider or a premium offering).

However, in saying all that, the following are some guidelines to help you decide.

EXCLUDE EVERYTHING THAT'S NOT INCLUDED—D'UH!

First up though, I want you to agree with me that you will NEVER ever list what's **EXCLUDED** on any of your agreements, quotes, plans and offerings.

You should ONLY ever draw up a list of what is **INCLUDED**.

And then, you should communicate strongly that **everything that is not included is excluded by default.**

While that last line is so simple, it's so darned important that I'm going to say it again.

Everything that is not included is excluded by default.

I have seen FAR too many MSPs have extremely uncomfortable conversations with their clients because the client believes a particular task they've just been billed for *should have* been included because it's not showing up in the list of exclusions the MSP sent through.

To avoid conversations like that, you simply need to make it as plain as day that you have an **Inclusion List,** and if it's not on there, **<u>it's not covered.</u>**

Now, I know I've just told you to never list what is **excluded** from your plans.

Well, I'm going to make a slight exception here. I have seen some MSPs include a page (either in their proposal template or on their website) that shows **examples** of things that **might be excluded.**

If you're going to do this (and it can be a good idea in certain industries)—then please make sure you word it similarly to the following so that there's absolutely no ambiguity:

"The way our Fixed Fee Support Agreements work is that whatever isn't covered in our Inclusion List is excluded by default. To help give you an idea about what might be excluded, here are some examples:

Example 1 (insert your own example here that is relatable to your clients)
Example 2 (insert your own example here that is relatable to your clients)
Example 3 (insert your own example here that is relatable to your clients)

From time to time, you might need us to help you out with something that's excluded from your Agreement and if/when that happens—we'll talk with you to understand the scope of the project so that we can deliver you a Fixed Price quote."

STACK, STACK AND THEN STACK

Make sure that your BETTER plan has **everything** from your GOOD plan (with some extras added on top) and that your BEST plan has **everything** from your BETTER plan (with even more added on top).

You'll see an example of this in my Plan Example in a later chapter with the way the Support Offerings are positioned.

- GOOD = Unlimited Business Hours Remote
- BETTER = GOOD + Unlimited Business Hours Onsite Support
- BEST = BETTER + Unlimited After-Hours Coverage.

If you make your plan differences more complex than this, you'll struggle to scale because your Agreements will be so darned complex, you'll spend all your time answering questions from your team and clients about them and have no time left for growing your business.

You need to make your plans EASY to understand for you, your team and your clients.

WHAT CAN AN INCLUSION LIST INCLUDE?

In terms of what to include in your plans, here are some ideas to get you started.

You can also grab this sample Inclusion List with some additional notes by downloading the **Resource Pack** that goes along with this book from packagepriceprofit.com/resources.

Desktop Support	Server Support	After Hours Support
24/7/365 Support	Emergency Support	Guaranteed Response Times
Incident Management	Mobile Device Management	Onsite Support (Business Hours)
Remote Support (Business Hours)	Vendor Management	Network Management
Incident Management	Security Incident Management	Asset Management
Business Continuity Planning	Adds/Moves/Changes	IT Budget Planning
Procurement Assistance	Documentation Management	Virtual CIO (Lite)
Virtual CIO (Standard)	Technology Business Reviews	Executive Reporting
Office365 Licenses	Virtual CIO (Premium)	G-Suite Licenses
Office365 Backup Licenses	Microsoft 365 Licenses	Server Backup
Simulated Disaster Recovery	Managed BDR	Penetration Testing
Simulated Phishing	Workstation Backup	Managed Anti-Malware
Managed Anti-Virus	Identity & Access Management	Managed Networking
Password Management	Managed Firewall	Vulnerability Scanning
Cybersecurity Awareness Training	Spam Filtering	Technology Enablement Sessions
Technology Adoption Sessions	End User Training	

Remember, less is often better here, and while some of this stuff is required for serving particular industries (e.g., financial or medical), lots of it isn't required, and so **<u>you should only include what you absolutely need to serve your clients and nothing more.</u>**

PRO TIP It's a great idea to include things in your agreements that are going to help lower your costs of delivering the service. An example here might be a **Managed Firewall.**

By including it, it means you will have centralized management of all your clients' firewalls from a single console, making it easy for you to roll out policies across all your clients to help block the latest Cybersecurity threat or Virus attack, eliminating any support tickets that might have been created from a successful attack coming through.

It might cost you slightly extra to include it in the Agreement; however, it can drastically lower your labor costs of supporting an agreement over the long term (if you include Virus Incident Remediation in your Agreements).

WHERE DO I SHOW THE INCLUSION LIST?

I recommend you include your Inclusion List either as an Appendix in your Managed Services Agreement or as a single point of reference on your website and refer to it regularly in conversations with clients.

You should only have one **Inclusion List** across ALL of your clients and offerings. Things get very messy and unscalable very fast if you try to have different Inclusion Lists across different offerings.

Shameless Plug: If you're looking for a good Managed Services Agreement template, we have one inside our Tech Tribe. Over a decade, I'd collected about 20 MSP Agreements from friends in the MSP space and pulled the best bits out of them to craft a world-class one.

Head to **https://thetechtribe.com/profitbook** for a special "readers only" offer to join our Tribe and immediately download the Template.

GUARANTEED RESPONSE TIMES

One of the main things most of your clients will judge your level of service on is **how fast you respond to them when they ask for help.**

This is often called a **Guaranteed Response Time** and is also often referred to as a Service Level Agreement or SLA (although in reality, an SLA encompasses many more things than just response times, so for the sake of making things simple, let's just focus on Guaranteed Response Times).

I typically encourage most MSPs to include **Guaranteed Response Times** in their plans; however, what I don't recommend (especially for Nimble MSPs like you) is having **different levels** of response times depending on the plan.

For example, having a 4-hour response time on your **Good** plan, a 2-hour response time on your **Better** plan and a 1-hour response time on your **Best** plan.

Even though the big PSA/Ticketing systems will allow for this, it just unnecessarily complicates the bejeepers out of your business and **sends the wrong message** about what you feel are priorities for clients.

In our end of the MSP space, where the Nimble MSPs play, your service delivery levels should ideally be the exact same across all of your plans.

There are two ways you can offer this.

1. **As a tiered guarantee**, depending on the severity of the problem.

It might look like this:

PRIORITY	EXAMPLES	GUARANTEED RESPONSE TIMES
CRITICAL	Your Main Server is offline and all users are unable to work.	1 Hour
	One of your Network Switches has failed and stopped half the company from working.	
	A VPN link between 2 x offices is offline causing one office to be unable to work.	
HIGH	Your Internet Connection is offline, users can still work locally	2 Hours
	Your CEO's computer has stopped working	
	Your main Accounting Software has stopped working	
MEDIUM	A user's desktop won't turn on so they can't work	4 Hours
	One of the main printers is not working, but users can print to another one	
	A user is having problems connecting to the Wireless network	
LOW	Printing is slower than normal	8 Hours
	A single user is unable to scan	
	A user needs a program installed on their PC	
NO PRIORITY	Pro-Active maintenance of systems	N/A
	Add / Edit / Delete User Requests	
	New Computer or Software Installation	

2. **As a single response time** but with escalation tiers behind the scenes.

It might look like this:

"Speak to an Engineer on the Phone in 60 Seconds or Less"

There are quite a few MSPs in the marketplace offering response times like this. It's a very compelling offer to a client and a great way to differentiate from everyone who's offering the first (slower) model.

If you aren't offering something similar, **you should consider it.**

Typically, the way it works is, you have your cheapest Level 1 Engineers answering the phones in a round-robin style approach, and then you have documented escalation processes so that they know when they should escalate an issue up to a Level 2, Level 3 or Senior Engineers.

Even for a **Nimble MSP** on the smaller scale, it's easier than ever to offer **near immediate response** with all the Outsourced NOC offerings available like Benchmark365, Collabrance, Continuum, GMS Live Expert, IT by Design, Mission Control, MSP Assist and NetEnrich.

(Outsourced NOC teams have really started to mature and gain traction around delivering a high-quality level of service, which is something they've traditionally struggled with for years.)

GUARANTEED RESOLUTION TIMES

Most **Nimble MSPs** aren't in a position to be able to offer **guarantees on resolving problems** because their clients' environments are often vastly out of their control, and the costs to make sure you can profitably offer a guarantee on resolution times are often completely prohibitive for SMB clients.

So, unless it's absolutely necessary in the industries and verticals that you serve (e.g., banking or medical), then you typically should stay away from resolution times and focus on **delivering awesome response times** instead.

In my 20 years in the industry, I've only ever had one client ask about resolution times, and when I explained about the costs required for us to be able to build their environment and the restrictions we'd need to put in place to offer Guaranteed *Resolution* Times, they nearly fainted and were more than happy to just stick with **Guaranteed <u>Response Times</u>**.

Sure, I'm painting with a pretty broad brush with this statement; however, remember that in this book I'm focusing on **Nimble MSPs**, and we're talking about the SMB market (not Enterprise where **Resolution** times are much more common). If you can figure out a way to **profitably guarantee Resolution Times** in low cost agreements in the SMB space without opening yourself up to unnecessary risk, then I say go for it. It can be another great differentiator. Just make sure that going to the trouble will be worth it.

WHAT SORT OF THINGS ARE EXCLUDED?

Well, this part is easy.

At our **All You Can Eat Buffet Restaurant** that we spoke about previously, if you felt like a **Kung Pao Chicken** and had walked around all the buffet stations and couldn't find one, then you could certainly go to your buffet hosts and ask them if they could make you one.

Your hosts will either say, **"Yep, we sure can—that'll be an extra $15,"** or they'll say, **"Sorry, we can't make that."**

And while it might upset you a little that you don't get to eat your favorite Kung Pao Chicken, you'll still be perfectly happy with both options and won't be upset at the hosts.

Because your expectation going into a buffet is that you can eat all you can fit inside your belly **<u>BUT ONLY FROM WHAT'S ON THE BUFFET.</u>**

The same goes with Unlimited IT Support Agreements and their Inclusion Lists (buffet).

Everything that isn't *included* in your **Inclusion List** is **Excluded by Default**.

And this is how you should always position things to your clients and prospects. We all know a buffet's not **truly** unlimited, and you should set that expectation with your clients as well.

We used the buffet example regularly when positioning things to our clients to make sure there were no grey areas.

If it's not on our Inclusion List, then by its very nature, it's **Excluded** and classed as **Out of Scope** work.

And all Out of Scope work should be offered on a **Pre-Paid Time & Materials** basis OR as a **Scope of Works with a Fixed Fee** (this second option is typically the best option but not always possible).

PRO TIP: I see too many **Nimble MSPs** scared of having a conversation with their clients whenever there's something that's **Out of Scope**.

Instead of telling their clients that whatever they want is not covered in their Agreement, they instead do it for free and not only rob themselves of healthy margin but also set a bad expectation that's hard to break for next time around.

If this is you—then just stop it. Please!

PRO TIP (Cont.):

The in scope/out of scope conversation happens every single day in many industries all around the world and it's a normal part of doing business. All good clients will understand and respect it, and the more conversations you have about it, the easier they become.

It took me a while on my journey to get comfortable with having the conversation with clients; however, I persisted. Eventually, clients started coming to us and saying things like, "I have an Out of Scope project I need your help on. Would you mind quoting it up for us?"

That's when I knew my continual conversations around **in scope** and **out of scope** had worked.

I encourage you to keep the conversation going with your clients, and you will also get to the same point where their expectations are right, and you don't blow away your margin.

CHAPTER 6

WILL OFFERING AYCE RUIN MY BUSINESS?

If you're still on the fence as to whether you should be offering some sort of Unlimited/All You Can Eat option inside your plans, then this section is for you.

It's funny, when I'm working with clients who are primarily offering Break/Fix services, one of the major reasons that they've never transitioned to an MSP or MRR model is that they're worried that their clients are going to abuse it and they're going to end up doing twice the amount of work for half the amount of money.

I say it's **funny**—because I've ONLY ever seen the opposite being true.

Hundreds of times.

Your clients wake up in the mornings wanting to design more buildings (architects), count more numbers (accountants) and fight more battles (our friendly lawyers).

They don't wake up and think, **"Oh, I'm going to put through an extra 10 requests to my IT support company today, just because I can."**

What often does happen though (which can be scary, if you don't know that it's perfectly normal), is that in the first 1–3 months after converting a Break/Fix client across to some sort of **Unlimited Support** offering is that their support requests will increase.

These initial requests are all the things that they've had piling up in the back of their head that they've wanted to ask for help with but haven't because they know it's going to cost them extra.

Now that they're on some form of **Unlimited Support**—they get all that low hanging fruit out of their heads.

It is perfectly normal, so make sure you expect it, and don't be scared off by it. After they get through their mental backlog, things will settle down and you'll see the **new normal.**

It's like our buffet restaurant example, people don't go there with a specific purpose of trying to send the restaurant broke.

They go there to get a food fix, and the restaurant knows how to satiate that hunger AND **make themselves a profit.**

CHAPTER 7

CAN I SEE AN EXAMPLE?

I'm sure you've been chomping at the bit to see some examples of how you **could** layout your plans.

So, if I was to be running an MSP today, in the marketplace that I used to work in (Sydney, Australia), knowing what I know now and being in the sub $5m space, my plans would likely look similar to the following:

> **NOTE:** As I mentioned earlier, you should not directly copy this as it will most likely fail for you. Instead customize it to work for you, your business, your marketplace and your clients.

THE TECH TRIBE	GOOD	BETTER	BEST
SUPPORT			
Guaranteed Response Times¹	☑	☑	☑
Bespoke Support Application	☑	☑	☑
Microsoft & 3rd Party App Updates	☑	☑	☑
Managed Anti-Virus / Anti-Malware	☑	☑	☑
24x7x365 Infrastructure Monitoring	☑	☑	☑
Managed Premium Firewall	☑	☑	☑
Unlimited Remote Support²	☑	☑	☑
Unlimited Onsite Support²	VIP Rates	☑	☑
Unlimited After Hours Support²	VIP Rates	VIP Rates	☑
SECURITY			
Password Management System	☑	☑	☑
Dark Web Monitoring	N/A	☑	☑
Simulated Phishing Attack	$1,495	Bi-Annual	Quarterly
Vulnerability Scan / Penetration Test	$2,995	Bi-Annual	Quarterly
MANAGEMENT			
IT Documentation	☑	☑	☑
Monthly Executive Report	☑	☑	☑
Asset & Inventory Management Report	$1,495	Annual	Bi-Annual
IT Budget Preparation	$2,495	Annual	Bi-Annual
Technology Business Review Meeting	Bi-Annual	Quarterly	Monthly
TRAINING			
Security Awareness Training	☑	☑	☑
End User Training	Billable	☑	☑
Technology Adoption Session	Bi-Annual	Quarterly	Monthly
SERVICES			
Office365 Enterprise License	☑	☑	☑
Office365 Backup License	☑	☑	☑
Monthly Human Backup Testing	☑	☑	☑
BDR as a Service	From $199/month	☑	☑
Simulated Mock BDR Test	Billable	Quarterly	Monthly
Per User Per Month	**$125**	**$150**	**$200**

1. You can find your Guaranteed Response Times (SLA) listed at yourcompanyname.com/fast
2. You can send in as many service requests as you like for any of the items in our Inclusion List

If you head to **https://packagepriceprofit.com/
resources** and download the resource pack, you'll be able
to grab the Excel version of this to play around with yourself. I've added another column to the downloadable version

where I explain WHY I have laid some things out the way I have.

Please keep in mind that the pricing here is completely arbitrary and is shown as an example only. Calculate your own numbers to put here, ideally based on the **Value-Based Pricing** model (we talk more about this below).

PRO TIP: In 99% of scenarios, you should never show your pricing publicly on your website or anywhere else that prospects or clients can see it. I have only listed the prices in the example above to give you an idea of how your pricing **could** look comparatively to each plan.

One of the only scenarios where you would list your pricing on your website would be if you have built a **high volume, low priced offering** that requires the client to sign up and onboard themselves (due to the skinny margins).

While this is a perfectly reasonable business model (and there are a few MSPs pursuing this model)—it's quite different to what we're talking about here, and so parts of this book won't apply.

PART III

WORKING OUT PRICING

CHAPTER 8

HOW DO I WORK OUT
MY PRICING?

Ahh, the perennial question. I thought you'd never ask. :-) So, first things first, let me tell you how you **shouldn't** set your pricing:

1. **You should NOT set your pricing based on your competitors pricing.**

Sure, it's good to know the basics of what your competitors charge so you know you're not **drastically** under or over charging in your marketplace.

However, the reality is that what your competitors are charging should only influence your pricing in a **very** minor way.

I often tell my coaching clients that they should care about their competition 500% less than what they currently do, and they should care about themselves, their own mindset and their own business improvements 500% more than what they currently do.

Unfortunately, it often starts out the opposite with them caring far more than they need to about their competition and nowhere near enough about themselves, their business and their mindset.

The reality is that you don't know anything about your competitors' business, their costs, the quality of their service, the tools they use to deliver the service, their Internal IP, the Automations they have developed or the types of clients they are targeting.

Heck, you don't even know whether they're even making any money at all!

If you operated in a highly commoditized and price-squeezed marketplace, like Telephony or Airlines, then sure, you need to focus more on worrying about your competitors' price as the vast majority of your clients will make the bulk of their decisions based on price.

However, you don't operate in a highly commoditized marketplace (more on that below), so sure, take some inspiration from your competitors (both locally and globally) about how they structure things, how they position offerings and even how they price things.

But don't base the BULK of your pricing decisions base off their pricing.

2. **You should NOT set your pricing while believing the market is heavily commoditized.**

Iron is one of the most (seemingly) commoditized items on the planet.

And in its rawest form—an iron bar—it sells for about $5.

However, turn that same $5 bar of iron into horseshoes, and it's now worth $12.

Now, what about if we turn that same amount of iron into needles?

It turns its value into $3,500.

Hmm... are you seeing what I'm seeing here?

Now, what happens if we turn that same $5 iron bar into springs for watches?

The value skyrockets to $300,000.

Sure, there are manufacturing costs and other items behind the scenes here, but I want you to **really, deeply** see the lesson here.

And that's that **Commoditized Businesses are often just a by-product of Commoditized Thinking** by the owner and leadership team.

As you're going through building your pricing, please do not fall victim to **Commoditized Thinking,** and instead focus on **Value Creation** as that's where the real money lies.

> **PRO TIP:** Value creation is turning a $5 bar of iron into $300,000.

The MSP Marketplace is NOT currently commoditized at all, and there are bucket loads of opportunity and money to be made in selling premium and high-level services positioned the right way.

Sure, some baseline offerings in the MSP world, like monitoring, maintenance and backups are (kinda) commoditized; however, things like **Managed Support, Managed Services, Technology Adoption, Technology Education, Technology Enablement and CyberSecurity** are far from being commoditized and likely won't be for a very, very long time (if at all).

There are too many variables across all the client requirements and environments around the world to even think that these things can be completely commoditized soon.

1. **You should NOT set your pricing based on licking a finger, throwing it up in the air and trying to work out which way the wind is blowing.**

You might have done this up in the past, and that might have also been OK for where your business journey was at the time.

However, now that you're reading this book—this is not the way to come up with your pricing.

In fact, the vast majority of us (me included for a long time) severely undervalue ourselves and don't charge enough, so this method is often the fastest road to ruin out there.

2. **You should NOT set your pricing on coming up with the PERFECT formula.**

As we discussed before, there is no perfect formula, and if you try to set your pricing this way, you'll never end up getting your offering in front of your clients.

HOW SHOULD YOU SET YOUR PRICING?

Right, so now we've run through how NOT to price your offering, let's now run through some of the most popular ways that you can set some pricing.

First up, please know that it's OK to experiment with your pricing; in fact, I'd like to go one step further and say that it's **mandatory** to experiment with your pricing.

Did you know that Amazon can change its product pricing up to 2.5 million times a day, making micro tests, experiments and adjustments to work out what prices work the best?

So, ideally you should follow Amazon's example and adjust your pricing at least 1 million times a day.

Kidding. :-)

But the reality is that business is far too fluid these days to set anything in stone for a long time, especially in the early stages of your pricing **maturity journey**.

This is one of the reasons why I mentioned earlier that **termed agreements** can be dangerous at a certain level of maturity in your MSP. If you lock a client into pricing that you later work out is wildly unprofitable, you could be locked into that **unprofitable** agreement for a long time (and trust me, that ain't no fun).

As I said earlier, it's not until you gain a good level of understanding of your costs and margins that you should think about putting contract lengths into your agreements.

The reality is that **how** you set your pricing is very heavily dependent on what stage your MSP is at on its journey of going through all the maturity levels. So, I'm going to run through all the methods being used by most MSPs around the world, and you can then decide what method you are going to use.

CHAPTER 9

THE DIFFERENT PRICING STRATEGIES

A s I mentioned in the beginning, I'm not going to fill this book up with information you can easily find on the Internet. So instead, I'm going to run through the most common ways to work out your pricing quickly, along with some behind the scenes/in the trenches thoughts on each one. You can then decide where you're at on your Maturity Journey, pick the model that works best for you and go and make it happen.

AVERAGE TRAILING 24 MONTHS

If you're currently doing a lot of Break/Fix or Ad-Hoc work and have no idea on what your clients might be going to use—then you might like to use this approach **to help kick off the transition to some sort of MRR/Managed Support or Managed Services.**

The easy way to handle this approach is to:

1. Print out a breakdown of your clients last 12–24 months service bills (don't include things like hardware and software or project work; you just need to know how much they spent on support costs over the trailing 12–24 months).

2. Check through them for any anomalies, and remove them (e.g., project work that was included that shouldn't have been).

3. Divide the total figure by 12 or 24 to come up with the average monthly figure.

4. Add as much to that figure as you can until it's uncomfortable for you (this is normally when it's getting to the right range).

5. Go to your clients and say, "Hey, we're making the shift away from lumpy ad-hoc pricing to make IT much more predictable and easier for you to budget for, and so we've averaged up your last 12 or 24 months spend and are happy to offer you $XXX for a fixed monthly fee."

Now, of course, this is <u>not a strategy for the long term</u>, as there are some inherent risks (especially if you don't have an **Inclusion List**), and you'll likely be missing out on lots of juicy margins for yourself!

However, like I said earlier, when you're just starting the transition from Break/Fix to MRR, **your focus should be on momentum, not perfection,** and if this strategy gets you into momentum, then I say **GO FOR IT!**

A bonus with this method is that it's an easy way to get your first 2–3 clients so you can honestly tell your other clients that you already have clients on **Fixed Fee Agreements** (this is great because it gives social proof that others have made the leap).

If you do use this approach, just make sure you watch your **Agreement Gross Margins** like a hawk to make sure no unprofitable agreements suck your business dry (more on that soon).

And aim to switch to **Value-Based Pricing** as fast as you can (more on that soon as well).

COST + MARKUP = PRICING

This is my least favorite way of seeing MSPs price their offering; however, it's currently the most common method (and admittedly one I used myself for a long time in my MSP).

The reason it's my least favorite is that it often ends up with you missing out on healthy margins as opposed to using a **Value-Based** approach (more shortly).

The way this model works is, you work out the cost of delivering the service (typically on a **Per User** basis), and then you throw a markup percentage on it and call it a day.

Cost + Markup pricing is typically OK when you're re-selling hardware and software, but it's not OK when you're pricing your highly valuable, expertise-driven, MSP offering.

If you were able to sit with your clients, stick a needle in their arm and inject them with some truth serum, you'll find that **most (if not all) of them would admit to being very happy to pay more for your services than they do now**.

(Of course, the big caveat here is that you need to be delivering them a great quality service, but you're already doing that, right? Right?)

So, please, don't use the Cost + Markup method to come up with your Agreement pricing.

VALUE-BASED PRICING

You've probably heard about **Value-Based Pricing**, but what the heck is it?

Value-Based Pricing is where you base your pricing primarily on the perceived or estimated value you bring to your clients rather than what it costs you to deliver the product or service.

Picture this: you're holding two t-shirts.

In your left hand, you have a white cotton crew neck t-shirt from a seller on Amazon.

In your right hand, you also have a white cotton crew neck t-shirt, but on the front of this one is the Adidas logo and the words RUN DMC in red (yes, RUN DMC the hip-hop group).

(Fun fact, I actually saw RUN DMC in concert in about 1998 and gave them all a high five when they came down to the front row. I didn't wash my hands for days.)

So, the t-shirt in your left hand has a price tag of $5.97.

The t-shirt in your right hand has a price tag of $13,000.

And no—it's not coated in gold liner and doesn't have any embedded diamonds. It's just a plain and simple white t-shirt with some lettering.

Both shirts cost about the same to build.

But their value is **VASTLY** different because the RUN DMC t-shirts' pricing is not based on what it cost.

The RUN DMC shirts' pricing is based on the **perceived value** of its buyer.

Multiple people paid $13,000 for this RUN DMC version of an Adidas t-shirt. Yep, crazy right?

And for every RUN DMC t-shirt sold, our poor Amazon seller has to sell, pack and ship 2,177 of their t-shirts.

And that, my friend, is **Value-Based Pricing**.

Now, you might have noticed on the back cover of this book, I've listed its value as $2,500.

Sure, I did it as a bit of a joke; however, I also did it to illustrate a serious point.

There are hundreds, if not thousands, of MSPs in the world that I could sit with and dig to find scenarios where they can use strategies or tactics in this book to **help them put hundreds of thousands of extra dollars in their bank account in the next 12 months.**

And if I positioned this book appropriately, they'd happily pay $2,500 to buy it.

Because the **tangible ROI** and value is there for them.

Here are some other reasons why **Value-Based Pricing** rocks:

1. It increases your profit margins (sometimes by a whopping amount).

2. It means you can work with less clients while making more money.

3. It gives you enough margin to help grow your business (It's easier to hire a team and invest in marketing when you have extra capital sitting there, right?).

4. It allows you to deliver AWESOME to your clients instead of just good (creating talking points and raving fans).

5. It aligns the value of your (and your team's) skills and knowledge with the value you bring the client (I know you're

worth more than you're currently earning.
Am I right?).

Although, let me warn you up front, switching to a **Value-Based Pricing** model in the MSP space can be tough. But it's oh so rewarding!

It requires building the confidence and skills to educate and show your prospects the **real tangible value** you <u>will</u> bring to them. And again, I'm not just talking about "Delivering Good IT Support" because that's not tangible, and it's certainly not differentiating.

Here are some steps to help you start the journey:

STEP 1: UNDERSTAND YOUR INTANGIBLES

Before you get started with **Value-Based Pricing**, you need to spend time making sure you really, truly have some things that separate you from your competition. These are often intangible, and so you can't put a price on them.

If I was to meet you at a conference and asked you, "Why is your MSP better than your competitor around the corner?" What would you say?

Here are some examples to give you some ideas:

- You are world-class at speaking in **business lingo** and not **geek speak**.

- You deeply understand the nuances of a particular niche after working in it for so long.

- You deeply understand certain platforms or software **better than anyone else**.

- You have a **unique experience** that means you can implement a certain solution far better than anyone else could.

- You can get a friendly tech answering calls in 60 seconds or less, 24/7/365.

- Your brand personality is fun, friendly, unique and stands out in a crowd.

- You've got raving fans in your marketplace who actually talk about you.

- You have intentional and unique ways of creating talking points with your clients.

If none of these apply to you and you can't immediately think of any of your own, then start creating some. If you don't, you'll always struggle to gain traction, differentiate yourself and charge what you really want.

STEP 2: STOP MENTIONING HOURS

For **Value-Based Pricing** to work, you need to stop doing hourly based work for clients, and you need to remove any mentions of hourly based pricing from everywhere you might have it (your Invoices, your Agreements, your Website, etc.).

In fact, do whatever you can to remove the word **hourly** out of your conversations completely. It doesn't have a place in the **Value-Based Pricing** model at all (unless you're talking to your clients about how many hours **THEY** will save with the Technology Solutions you deliver them).

STEP 3: FIND THE PROSPECTS' PAIN AND OPPORTUNITIES

This is where the bulk of the work happens. Here, you work with your prospect to find and understand their biggest pains and opportunities that you are uniquely positioned to solve for them.

Here are some trigger questions you can use in this process to help you uncover some juicy information:

- If you could wave a magic wand and immediately solve a Technology problem in your business that's driving you stark raving mad—what would it be?

- What frustrates you the most with your IT?

- What would happen if your sensitive data was stolen?

- Where do you feel like you could be using Technology better?

- What are the things that scare you the most with your Technology?

- What does it cost your business per hour when your computers are offline? (You can walk them through the process of working out this number.)

- What is your current RTO & RPO? (Yep, this question will leave most prospects scratching their heads wondering what it means, and that's perfect because then you drop in a few minutes of education around what those metrics mean to them and how they can impact them—positioning you as an authority.)

- What are you currently spending on IT? (This one might seem simple and perhaps a little intrusive; however, it can deliver some gold.)

One of my favorite coaching clients asked a prospect the **IT Spend** question in a recent sales call and found out that they were currently paying about $12,000 per month for outsourced IT Support for only 25 users (yeah, crazy right?).

If he hadn't asked the question and just used his old pricing model, he would have quoted them about $2,000 per month for IT Support.

Instead, he had his first go at **Value-Based Pricing** and added another 50% to his normal price and charged them $3,000 a month, closing the deal immediately with an ecstatic client who's saving a tidy sum each month.

He's still vastly undervaluing himself, but that's OK—he's on a journey and has climbed up a rung on the confidence ladder using the **Value-Based Pricing** model so next time he comes across an opportunity like this, he won't be afraid to go even higher!

Once you find some threads to start digging deeper into, you can use probing questions like these to find the real value of these **pains and opportunities**:

- What would it mean to you if you solved that problem?
- How many hours a week would that save you?

- How long have you been wanting to solve this problem?

- What's it worth to you to spend your weekends not worrying about that issue?

- How much is that costing you each month?

- How many hours are you wasting on that one?

- Are you willing to make an investment in fixing this for good?

- How soon are you prepared to take action?

- If you don't solve this problem, what will this cost you?

- If this happens, what will this cost you?

- If you don't take this opportunity, what will this cost you?

Gathering all this data will help you paint a picture of where to focus to get them their most valuable results.

Sure, this type of work will make the **Value-Based** selling process **a little longer** than what you might be used to—but trust me, the little bit of extra time up-front is worth it for those healthy extra margins over the long term!

STEP 4: SELL THE SOLUTIONS
Good work, you've now done the hard work of uncovering and deeply understanding your clients' pain points and opportunities, and now it's time to line them up with your solutions!

This is not a slimy, icky, used-car salesman process.

Your whole job here is to:

1. Communicate to them what you've uncovered in the last step, highlighting the potential returns or costs of inaction.

2. Explain how any of your Intangibles will impact things (perhaps your **60-Second Response Time Guarantee** or your **Sleep Soundly Data-Safe Program**).

3. Walk them through your Solution(s)— often this will mean walking them through your Agreement or your Good/ Better/Best offerings, paying particular attention on the parts that solve their biggest, highest ROI pain points you uncovered in the last step.

You shouldn't talk about **your** pricing at this point yet.

You should be showing them the returns they will get working with you and what the cost could be if they choose not to. You need to quantify these amounts into something tangible (honestly and realistically, of course, we aren't selling snake oil here).

This is where you want to get buy-in from the client on your solution. You want them nodding their head saying, "Yep, gimme some of that goodness."

If you're not getting that yet—you need to do some more work.

Once you have buy-in on your solution and the nodding head—move on to the next step.

PRO TIP: If a prospect pushes you for price here, simply reply with:

"While I'd love to give you a price right now, we need to first work out what solution is going to solve your problems. I promise as soon as we've done that, we can then figure out pricing."

It's a very respectful way to answer the pricing question and stay in control of the conversation.

STEP 5: PRICE IT AND CLOSE IT

So, you're probably now asking, "How the heck do I work out this perceived or estimated value in the Value-Based Pricing model?"

Well, great question, my friend...

And the answer is that there is **no definitive answer.**

Sorry to disappoint, but I warned you right at the very beginning of the book that there is no secret formula here that works for everyone.

Arriving at a price in a **Value-Based Pricing** model is **more art than science.**

It's a never-ending journey you go on. As your confidence grows using the model, your ability to increase the amount you charge grows with it.

However, in saying that, an approach that can help you as you're starting out is to use the 10% rule.

For example, if I'm able to demonstrate that I can deliver $40,000 of value per month to a client, I might start my pricing at $4,000 per month for my GOOD plan, $5,000 for my BETTER plan and $7,000 for my best plan.

How on earth do I demonstrate $40,000 worth of value you might ask?

Well, here are some idea starters:

- Giving the owner their nights and weekends back so they can spend it with their kids instead of fixing computer issues for their staff—VALUE $10,000 per month

- Helping the owner sleep soundly at night, knowing all their confidential clients' data in their $45 million dollar a year business is protected and available—VALUE $10,000 per month

- Reducing the inefficiency of email overwhelm across the company by 30%—VALUE $6,000 per month

- Helping them reduce their head count by two full time admin people—VALUE $16,000 per month

- Getting rid of the slow and crashing computers that are causing lost work and frustrated morale—VALUE $4,000 per month

- Protecting against Ransomware Threats that could take the entire business in its current form out of action for 3 days—$10,000 per month peace of mind

Sure, these all might sound completely arbitrary. However, they are also **very real** scenarios in **many** businesses out there.

Heck, I'd **personally** pay $10,000 per month just to make sure that I had my nights and weekends free with my kids.

And in my small business, I'd happily pay $5,000 per month to know without a shadow of a doubt that my clients' data is all safe, secure and protected.

What would you pay for those two?

Value-Based Pricing is not about the time you spend; it's about the outcomes you deliver.

What you're selling here is peace of mind, extra family time, a competitive advantage, a way to innovate faster and a higher status amongst peers. This stuff is **VALUABLE**.

The better you understand the ROI, opportunity costs, business costs and how much your prospects value these things—the easier it becomes to come up with (realistic) prices. And the more you do it, the better you get at it.

STEP 6: OVERCOME OBJECTIONS, NEGOTIATE AND RE-CLOSE

Hopefully by now, you've already closed the deal and are explaining the next steps of the onboarding journey to the client. Kudos, if so!

However, there's also a chance that you haven't closed them just yet, especially if you're just starting out on your Value-Based journey and getting used to the process.

If your prospect has objections here, obviously you should work to overcome those objections. This might mean that you need to dive deeper into some of the intangibles or tangibles to get them framing things the right way.

Or perhaps you might need to dive deeper into their particular objection to find the root cause, and then see if you can build an ROI model out of solving that particular issue to create some tangible numbers to work from.

If you haven't been able to close them still and you feel like they really need what you have, they just don't realize it yet—then you can either negotiate on features (if possible) or price (not ideal, but not the end of the world with Value-Based Pricing).

As I've spoken about a few times so far in this book—as you mature through your Value-Based Pricing journey, you will likely get to the point where you only offer one plan/offering to your prospects instead of presenting three options (GOOD/BETTER/BEST).

If this is the case, then you may be able to down-sell them to what would be your unadvertised GOOD or BETTER plans (because your one plan would be your BEST plan). This would mean they'll get less features.

> **WARNING**: Don't chop apart your plans to try and create a bespoke plan for someone though; this will make your business very unscalable and complex. You want to have the same offerings across all your clients, even if some of those offerings are unadvertised.

Otherwise, if you really need to—then negotiate on price.

Remember, you've likely priced this agreement far higher than what you traditionally would have, so there is going to be some wiggle room.

But promise me that if you do get to the point that you're going to negotiate on price, please don't do it in a desperate way.

Instead, look for ways to close your prospect in a respectful and non-desperate way.

One of my suppliers closed me just like this recently, and here's how they did it:

I had spoken to them about a project that was going to cost me around $10,000. We'd been on a phone call; they'd understood my pains, and they'd presented their GOOD/BETTER/BEST offerings to me.

I liked their options, and I knew I wanted to work with them. However, life and other projects got in the way, and I just didn't prioritize signing on the dotted line.

Low and behold, two weeks later, I received an email in my inbox from my supplier saying that it was his birthday that week, and to celebrate he's taking 10% off anyone who signs a proposal by 5pm COB a few days later.

Boom—I signed before the deadline.

I knew I wanted to work with him, I simply needed the extra (respectful) shove to get me to make the decision.

Value Based Pricing for Projects

Value-Based Pricing isn't just reserved for your **Ongoing Agreements** with clients—it also works **perfectly** for Project Work.

In fact, it's often easier to use **Value-Based Pricing** with Projects than it is with Ongoing Agreements, especially when that project work includes some kind of Business Improvement Project.

For example, let's say one of your clients is a law firm of 50 staff, made up of lawyers, paralegals and support staff.

One day while you're at their office running a Technology Business Review session with the Managing Partner (I'll explain what that is shortly), you ask them one simple question:

"If you could wave a magic wand and immediately solve a technology problem in your business that's driving you stark raving mad—what would it be?"

The Managing Partner replies and says that emails are driving him and his team crazy, and everyone's getting overwhelmed.

You bounce back with a few probing questions, digging deeper, and you uncover that the entire business sends the majority of their contracts and documents internally to each other via email all day, every day causing the (expensive) paralegals to perform loads of double handling, troubleshooting versioning issues and tracking down where the right document is.

It drives the Partner mad, seeing all the **waste and inefficiency.**

He's not stupid though; he knows there's a better way.

He just doesn't have the time or skills to work it out because he's far too busy charging $400 per hour fighting in courtrooms (Lawyers love a good fight, don't they?).

Scenarios like this are so common. They exist everywhere, in your business, in my business; in fact, if you dig, **you'll find scenarios like this in every single business in the world.** It just takes a little digging.

So, you mention to the Partner that they already have the Technology to make this process far more efficient, much faster AND far less prone to errors and mistakes. They just aren't using it yet.

You briefly walk them through some back-of-the-napkin numbers.

Let's say on average, each of their 20 paralegals wastes a measly (and ultraconservative) 12 minutes on a typical day saving documents from emails, attaching documents to emails, sending emails asking people to review a document, fixing up mistakes because the wrong copy was sent, trying to find copies of contracts and comparing all the multiple copies in email chains to find the right one.

12 minutes a day multiplied by those 20 paralegals is 240 minutes wasted a day.

In a 5-day week, that's 1,200 minutes.

And monthly, that's a whopping 5,200 minutes, which is 86 hours!

That's 86 hours of wasted time every single month that you've uncovered, just from their paralegals and just with this one particular problem.

Now, let's say that the average hourly cost of their paralegals to their business is $60 (again, being conservative).

The 86 hours of wasted time at an average cost of $60 per hour = $5,160 per month!

That's $61,920 per year!

And that's just the raw cost—not even the opportunity cost!

If they fix this problem, they could reduce their head count by one full-time paralegal, or even better, redirect all that wasted time into other higher revenue generating activities, like building out a new productized offering for their own clients.

Now, you **could** then say:

"Ok, we could set up Sharepoint for you so you can do document collaboration, and we'll configure and install Microsoft Teams, which you should use to help cut down on some of your Email Chatter. It'll take us about 10 hours to configure Sharepoint and get Teams set up so we'll be able to do the project for around $1,200 to $1,500. Is that OK?"

OR you could start of by realizing that:

You are solving a $61,920 per year problem here that can only be uniquely solved well by you and your team because of your combined decades of industry experience with law firms coupled with your intimate knowledge of them and their team.

So, instead, you say to them:

"Ok, we can easily bring you a minimum of $60,000 worth of efficiencies (or real savings) to your bottom line every single year here by helping you better use existing Technology you already have.

"We'll plan out and build you a bespoke structure in your existing **Sharepoint** that mirrors your business structure, using our unique **Law-Firm SharePoint Onramp** process so we can get everyone on the same page, collaborating on documents in a central location with no mistakes, missing documents or version problems ever again.

"Then, we'll set up and implement **Microsoft Teams** across the firm (including on mobiles) to reduce your crazy email overwhelm by at least 20% and likely MUCH more.

"We'll connect everything together so that everyone works from a single pane of glass giving you even more efficiency.

"During this process, we'll run 3 onsite training sessions with your team to get everyone up to speed, and then we'll phase this implementation over 3 months, starting with the Accounting team first so you get comfortable with a smaller team first.

"We'll be on hand for unlimited help with anything related to the project for 60 days afterwards, and we'll write you up a short, sharp user manual so that anyone new joining the firm can get up to speed really quickly!

"The investment will be $15,000, and we'll have it done by the end of July. Here are the payment terms."

BOOM!

You've dug for pain, you've agitated it, you've crafted a solution, you've showed confidence, you've then linked it to a **tangible** ROI and you're giving it to them at a steal of a price (only 25% of their annual savings from just the first year alone (Try getting those returns from a bank!).

And in the process, you've made yourself **10 times more** than what you could have with the first option, with roughly the exact same project.

Plus, as an added bonus, because you've come across FAR more confidently and impressed the Managing Partner by approaching this from a **Business Perspective** rather than from a **Technology Perspective**, they immediately start thinking of other inefficiency issues in their business that you can help them solve with Technology.

And this, my fellow tech geek friend, is how to use **Value-Based Pricing** with Project work.

Trust me; you will feel uncomfortable with it at first. Heck, it might even feel like you're taking advantage of your client. Trust me; you aren't. This entire process is voluntary. You're operating in a free market.

If you execute well, the Managing Partner is singing your praises because you've not only solved his most frustrating problem, you've also got him a tangible ROI on his investment in only 3 months' time.

Once he says YES to your request for a Case Study, you end up with even more ammo to go and close the next similar deal at $20,000 or even $30,000.

Heck, I guarantee you there are law firms out there who would happily pay $60,000 (100%) for a project like that, knowing all too well that they are going to be making BUCKET loads of ROI on that investment from the second year onwards.

The more clients and projects you land at higher and higher prices using **Value-Based Pricing**, the more your confidence grows and the more you'll start earning what you know deep down inside that you're really worth.

(Go and read that last paragraph again—they're probably the most important words in this entire book. There are literally millions and billions of dollars of opportunity in there.)

Once you get some momentum going with **Value-Based Pricing**, you'll wonder why the heck you ever used any other model, and you might even start to look at using it with other things like **Product Resale** (although that's a topic for another day).

What's a Technology Business Review?

Most MSPs call these **Quarterly Business Reviews** (or QBR's). However, I prefer to call them **Technology Business Reviews** (or TBR's), as there is no rule that says they have to be done quarterly.

With your bigger clients it might be better to have them monthly, and with your smaller clients you might only need to sit with them once or twice a year.

(I wish I could take credit for this idea; however, one of our legendary Tech Tribers, Chris Moroz, was the one who mentioned it to me.)

THE OPPORTUNITY IS RIDICULOUS!

Now, I've used a conservative example here with our lawyer friends with a potential time saving of only 60 minutes (or 1 hour a week) for a sub-set of staff.

In June 2019, the research firm, Insight, performed a study across 2,000 UK office workers and found that on average, each person they surveyed admitted to wasting approximately 2.4 hours each week because they don't have the right technological support and tools.

Yes, you read that right—the average is 250% more than what I used in our conservative law firm example.

And, at least 20% of the workers claimed that they waste between 3 and 8 hours!

Extrapolated up across all the businesses in the UK, this amounts to 1.8 billion working hours wasted each and every year.

Or, as I like to see it—1.8 billion opportunities, just in the UK alone.

There are LOADS of managers and business owners desperate to solve these problems and they need your help!

It's a modern-day gold rush!

The more you practice spotting these opportunities and the more you skill yourself up to be able to sell the value to prospects and clients, the more people you'll be able to help and obviously, the more money you'll make.

And, when the economy has its next inevitable downturn (yes, it will happen), you'll be extremely well positioned to help all the businesses who are looking to cut costs and get more from their dollars.

WORKING WITH GOOD/BETTER/BEST

Despite what some might say, the **Value-Based Pricing** model can work well with the Good/ Better/Best model, as you can get the best of both worlds.

You get high, sustainable margins and the benefits of price anchoring, and your prospects still get the experience of going **shopping and feeling like they're in control.**

Once your prospect is at a place in the sales journey where they truly understand the costs to the business of the problems you've uncovered with them, then BOOM.

You present them your solution using a Good/Better/ Best strategy that solves their problem and give them tangible ROI with three powerful, profitable choices.

Your prospect still gets that feeling of shopping that we spoke about before, but you get the margins that you want and deserve.

This approach isn't for everyone, so experiment and see how it feels for you.

CHAPTER 10

WHAT ARE MY COSTS?

Each agreement you have with your clients will have an inherent cost to you to deliver each month (or quarter).

The cost to deliver an agreement is made up of your labor costs (you and your team) plus any additional product or service offerings you have bundled in (e.g., Anti-Virus licensing).

And while you've seen in the last chapter that I don't recommend simply adding a markup to your Agreement costs to determine your Plan pricing, I do recommend you have a basic understanding of your baseline costs of delivering your Agreements to make sure what you're delivering is profitable and sustainable and to keep an eye out for any negative trends and opportunities for more margin.

The formula to calculate your costs to deliver an agreement is actually quite simple:

**Labor Costs + Product/Service Costs =
Total Agreement Costs**

Let's dive real quick into how you calculate each of them.

LABOR COSTS

You might have heard the term **Fully Burdened Labor Rate**. This is essentially how much it costs your business, on a per hour basis, to have one of your billable team members (or you) sitting at a desk (or in a car or at a client's office) ready to help your clients.

It's basically calculated with a formula that starts with your engineer's base salary, then adds any additional costs (such as superannuation or 401K), does some calculations around averages for typical engineer availability (due to things like sickness, holidays) and then finally chucks in a proportion of the unbillable expenses in your business (e.g., admin staff, office rent, insurances, etc.).

What pops out of the calculation is a number that is the approximate cost of that person for that hour to the business, fully burdened.

I'm not going to bore you in this book with the intricate details of how to calculate this number as there are some great **Burden Rate Calculators** available online to help you. Simply search for "MSP Fully Burdened Labor Rate Calculator" and take a look through a few.

You should calculate a number for each role (or person) in your business and enter that number against each team member in your PSA Tool so it calculates your Agreement Gross Margin using the right costs.

My biggest encouragement here is to NOT get caught up in making this calculation perfect as it's not possible to get it completely accurate.

The main thing you're looking for with the data you get out of knowing this cost, is a TREND. So as long as you are consistent with your formula, it doesn't matter (much) if it's not 100% accurate. What matters more is that you spot trends and investigate them (more on that shortly).

PRODUCT/SERVICE COSTS

This part is **much easier**.

You simply include any costs of products or services that you have bundled into your plans. In a PSA Tool, this is often done by adding Agreement Products.

For example, if you're going to include an Office365 License, then add it into your Agreement as an included product with its appropriate costs (most PSA Tools allow this). If you're going to include things like 3rd Party Office365 Backups, then do the same thing.

It's wise to add a buffer on these costs (perhaps 10–20%) to account for things like currency fluctuations, pricing breaks and other things that make the price move up and down over time.

Better to understate your expected profits rather than overstate them, right?

If you think this sounds too simple, the reality is that **it is simple**.

Too many MSPs overcomplicate this stuff and end up spending far too much time here, trying to get things perfect—when their competition is out there closing deals and taking clients knowing that their understanding of their costs is **rough but enough.**

CHAPTER 11

MONITORING AGREEMENT GROSS MARGINS

O nce you have worked out your costs of delivering your Labor and your Products on your Agreements and entered these costs into your PSA tool, then you can now monitor how much profit you are making on your agreements on a month to month (or quarter to quarter) basis.

This is called your **Agreement Gross Margin Percentage** and depicts the profit margin percentage on that Agreement based on the Gross Revenue that the agreement brought in.

You can calculate this number by using one of the most underutilized reports in most PSA Tools, the **Agreement Gross Margin Report**.

The problem is that most PSA Tools (at the time of writing) unfortunately don't offer an **historical** version of this report, which is where the juicy information lies.

It's all good and well to understand how much profit you have made from your agreements over the last month. However, you can't really do anything with that data unless you are comparing it with previous reporting periods to spot trends and make amends.

So, what I recommend you do every month is to print out your **Agreement Gross Margin Report,** and then manually enter the numbers from that report into a separate rolling spreadsheet that looks like this:

	Rogue Fuel	Estate Storm	Cedar Home LLC	Month Average
January	62.3%	58.5%	55.5%	58.8%
February	62.5%	55.8%	48.2%	55.5%
March	55.3%	61.3%	52.3%	56.3%
April	48.7%	60.9%	56.4%	55.3%
May	49.2%	58.7%	57.8%	55.2%
June	47.4%	59.2%	59.3%	55.3%
July	42.2%	63.4%	64.2%	56.6%
Client Average	52.5%	59.7%	56.2%	

(You can download this Excel Template in the Resource pack to help you get started by heading to packagepriceprofit. com/resources.)

Across the top, you list all your clients (adding a new column whenever you get a new client), and down the left-hand side you list the months (some people prefer to use quarters; however, I'm a monthly guy myself).

You'd typically see a report like this done with your clients down the left hand side and the time periods across the top; however, I like it the opposite in this report because having all your clients across the top makes it **much easier to spot trends** with the colored Conditional Data Bars.

As you can see in our example above, we have a bit of a problem with **Rogue Fuel** as they're getting progressively more unprofitable, and so you need to do some root cause analysis to work out what the heck is going on with them (you should have been investigating this issue MUCH earlier than July—I've just made the example clearly to emphasize the point).

In most cases the underlying root cause is one (or more) of the following:

1. The client needs to invest in some newer infrastructure, and the MSP has been letting them get away with not doing it (at their expense).

2. The MSP is giving away too much free work that should have been classed as **Out of Scope** (remember, we spoke about that earlier).

3. The Agreement has been badly priced and needs renegotiation (which is perfectly OK —what's the point of having an unprofitable agreement sucking your business dry; you might as well either renegotiate or drop the client).

NOTE: If you're the business owner, you shouldn't be the one collating this report. This is a very easy process to create a Standard Operating Procedure (SOP) for and have someone else on your team perform.

It doesn't have to be your bookkeeper or someone in the financial; it can simply be a recurring ticket on your help desk for one of your techs to prepare each month.

Most MSPs average around 35%–55% gross margins from their Agreements; however, **Best in Class MSPs** (as Paul Dippell calls them) who are at a high Operational Maturity Level often see between 60%–80% gross margins from their Agreements.

And if you get really good at Value Based Pricing like I spoke about above, you might be able to find even more.

I have seen so many MSPs (myself included) have very uncomfortable realizations once they start monitoring their gross margins, often giving them a very different perspective who their best and worst clients really are (hint: it's often the opposite of what you think).

CHAPTER 12

SHOULD I CHARGE A SETUP FEE?

A common question I see asked in the MSP space is whether to charge new clients a setup fee when they sign up to a **Managed Services or Support Agreement.**

And like other questions, there is **no right or wrong answer here** as it typically comes down to where you are on your journey and what Operational Maturity Level your MSP is at.

My recommendation though is to **always show** a Setup Fee.

Whether you charge it or not can be dependent on a few things.

For example, if you are in a competitive sales scenario and you get a sense that charging the setup fee might be the one thing that means your prospect will go with one of the competitors, then you can likely discount it, knowing full well that you'll make it back very quickly once you start working deeper with the client.

However, you should still **show** it (but discounted to zero) on all the Proposals, Agreements and Invoices because the reality is that it costs money to onboard a new client, and you want to show your new clients that onboarding them has a value attached to it and to help set an expectation around what that value is.

You need to set them up in your systems. You need to grab all their (likely horrible) documentation from the incumbent provider, and document it in your (hopefully awesome) documentation system. You need to roll out your RMM tool, perhaps also your preferred firewall & A/V, your security policies and likely much more.

SIDE NOTE: In competitive scenarios, if you're getting squeezed for price, do whatever you can to not drop your actual monthly charge. Instead, either down-sell them to a plan that includes less (perhaps an unadvertised plan, like we spoke about before) OR walk away.

If you ever feel like you're being forced to drop your margins on your Agreement to the point where you can't deliver an awesome level of service and you can't properly protect and manage your client's business—then walk away.

There's no point competing so aggressively on price (in our "uncommoditized" industry) and then being forced to deliver an unprofitable and dangerous level of service.

Whoever does that is going to either go out of business first or screw up their clients' technology so badly that their clients will go out of business.

Another reason you might consider discounting the set-up fee is if you're locking people into long term contracted agreements (3+ years). You should **still** tell your clients you have a setup fee (and show them on Proposals, Agreements and Invoices), but offer to waive it because of the guaranteed contract length.

My preference here is to **still charge a setup fee** so you have enough margin to deliver your new clients an **AWE-SOME** onboarding experience that'll not only keep them around for many years to come (contract or not) but will have them raving about you to their friends.

CHAPTER 13

PRICING FOR AWESOME

One of the easiest ways to differentiate yourself from your competition and stand out in your marketplace is to **deliver an offering to your clients that is so ridiculously awesome that they can't help but tell their friends and colleagues.**

Now, I'm not just talking about being fast and friendly at closing tickets.

Every MSP already does that (or so they say).

In his great (short) book, **GIFT·OLOGY**, John Ruhlin recommends setting aside between 2% and 8% of the total profits from a client and investing that back into the relationship as a way to be intentional about creating those raving fans and **really** help them know that you love, appreciate and value the heck outta them.

Not in a self-serving way where you send them free pens, laptop bags or hats with **your** logo on it. Everyone knows that's just sneakily promoting your own brand.

I'm talking about loving on them in the same way you might love on a close family member or friend when it's their birthday and you want them to feel extra special.

Perhaps it's sending them and their significant other out to a fine-dining restaurant for their birthday. Or even better, perhaps it's gifting them a set of high-quality Japanese Steak Knives engraved with their family name for their Anniversary of when they started working with you.

(John talks deeper about this Knife example in the book. It's an excellent example because it creates a talking point whenever they have guests over for dinner and use knives. They get to share about their awesome IT company that they received them from.)

John shares another amazing story in the book.

He had been trying to talk to Cameron Herold, the COO of 1-800-GOT-JUNK to see if he could do some business with their company.

One day he managed to get on a brief call with Cameron and discovered that he was going to be visiting John's city soon and hoped to do some clothes shopping on his trip.

Thinking quickly, John asked for Cameron's shirt size so he could send him one of his favorite shirts and then offered to take him to dinner and a basketball game while he was in town. Cameron said yes!

On the day Cameron was due to arrive, John learnt that his plane was delayed and he'll likely miss out on his clothes shopping time. Thinking quickly again, John headed to the local Brooks Brothers store and purchased one of everything. $7,000 worth!

He then worked with Cameron's hotel to set his room up like a mini Brooks Brother store so once Cameron arrived in town, he could quickly and easily pick some new clothes before heading out to the basketball game.

Cameron was blown away saying "Whatever you want to talk about for as long as you want to talk about it, I'm all in! I've never had anybody treat me this way...".

Fast forward 9 years later and Cameron has invited John to his 50th birthday party and his wedding and has mentioned John from stages all over the world.

But most importantly, he's opened up doors with the president of Starbucks and some of the biggest companies in the world resulting in millions in new revenue for John.

What awesome gift ideas can you come up with for your clients and prospects?

I challenge you to make sure you've got enough margins in your offerings to be able to intentionally create AWESOME talking points like this. Do whatever you can to blow your clients' socks off with love. Get them addicted to working with you, and you'll never have to worry about your competition again.

PART IV

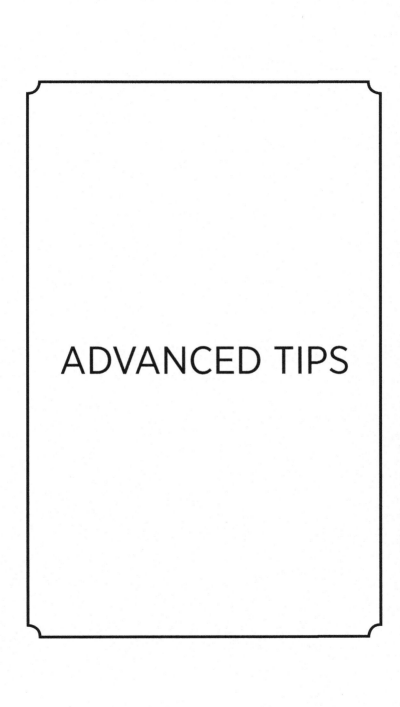

ADVANCED TIPS

CHAPTER 14

SHOULD I LOCK CLIENTS IN CONTRACTS?

There is a lot of debate in the industry on this topic. There are MSPs and MSP Coaches out there who will tell you that you're an idiot if you don't lock your clients into a termed agreement.

And there are other MSPs and MSP Coaches out there who tell you the exact opposite and say that you should differentiate yourself by having a 30-day out clause (meaning your clients can cancel their service with you with only 30 days' notice, and you can do the same to them).

The reality is that both sides of the debate are right (at times), and both are wrong (at times). And it's perfectly OK for you to choose whatever option you'd like, **as long as you understand and are happy with the pros and cons of the decision you've made.**

Two of the main things to keep in mind when making your decision around whether you should put contract lengths on your agreements are:

1. How good you are at the sales process; and

2. How much you care about getting the absolute maximum valuation of your MSP when you exit it (and let's face it—you **will** be exiting your business one day).

The reality I see is that a lot of **Nimble MSPs**, especially those doing less than $1 million in annual revenue, don't have a highly mature sales process (yet) and don't intimately understand their costs (yet), and so locking themselves into a termed, contracted agreement with their clients (that's potentially unprofitable) can be **very dangerous.**

Plus, obviously it's **easier** to get a prospect to sign an agreement if you can tell them that they can get out of that agreement in only 30 days as opposed to 1,095 days (the most common termed contract in the MSP space).

As I spoke about before, in the lower maturity levels of your MSP journey, it's often much more important to get clients in the door than it is to worry about whether you're locking them into multi-year contracts or not (you can always do that at a later date).

I was speaking at an MSP event in London recently, and one of the MSP owners there (a smart MSP dude named Tim) mentioned in a session that he has an average contract length of 6.25 years. Yes, 6.25 YEARS!

Tim's sales process in his MSP is **very mature**, and he has an **intricate understanding** of his costs, so it's perfectly OK for him to do this. You can get there as well.

FUN FACT: When my MSP was acquired in 2016, we went through an anonymous pre-diligence process with about 35 MSPs that were interested in buying us. What surprised me the most through the process was that **only** about 50% of the buyers asked us whether our agreements were termed or not.

And the MSP who ended up buying us, didn't ask whether our agreements were termed at all (and they paid a great price comparatively against the MSPs who did ask).

Goes to show that Termed Agreements, while important, aren't the be-all and end-all.

So, my encouragement to you is this. If you're just starting out in your MSP journey, if you don't feel like you're amazing at the sales process, if you don't feel comfortable signing clients up to termed agreements, then don't.

It's as simple as that and it's OK. Know though, that you're likely reducing the valuation of your MSP—and often that's OK as well.

However, once you get to a certain point in your journey (or if you're there already) where you are very confident in your sales process and understand your costs very well, then please think strongly about terming your agreements—both for your own valuation and for your clients' peace of mind.

MID-TIER CLIENTS: If you end up working with clients in the mid-market space (100–1,000 seats), the dynamics change a little as mid-market clients often want a termed contract.

Yep, you read that right. Mid-market clients often want (and are sometimes required) to be locked into an agreement, so they know their costs are fixed for a certain period of time, they are getting the best deal and that they don't have to change IT providers for a number of years (which can be very costly for a bigger business).

Keep this in mind when working in the mid-market space.

CHAPTER 15

GIVING AWAY FREE WORK

From time to time, you will likely want to give some work away for free to a client.

Maybe you're feeling particularly generous that day, maybe your client deserves it or maybe you're about to send them a big proposal soon and you want them to feel EXTRA special about working with you before you submit it.

Whatever the reason, whenever you do this, I want you to promise me that you will **always** show the client the VALUE of the work you just delivered.

A great way to be able to do this is by issuing **a zero-dollar invoice** showing the full amount of the free work you or your team performed with a corresponding discount line on the Invoice that makes the Invoice = $0. Most PSA tools make this very easy.

This does 3 things:

1. It reminds the client of the value of something that they might not have seen the true value of.

2. It helps set the expectation that you likely will bill for that type of work in the future.

3. If you set the parameters of the Ticket correctly in your PSA so that it's **FREE** but **NOT** associated with the clients' Fixed Price Agreement, this work won't incorrectly skew your **Gross Margin Agreement reports** (this is more important than you might initially think as you scale up).

CHAPTER 16

HOW DO I DEAL WITH COMPLEX CLIENTS?

W e've all had them. That client with only 10 staff but 5 Virtual Servers. Or that CFO who forces you to write a 15-page proposal to justify every single project you deliver for them.

Complexity exists everywhere. In infrastructure, in business models, in relationships and expectations.

And this complexity makes it extremely hard for us to standardize on a pricing model that suits all types of prospects that come our way.

So, unless you're fully migrated across to the **Value-Based Pricing** model I mentioned earlier, the easiest way I've found to overcome this that doesn't introduce even more unnecessary complexity, is to include a weighting factor when working out your pricing for a client.

So, if you have a new prospect that comes your way that has those 10 staff but has 5 Virtual Servers, and for whatever reason the type of business that they are means that they absolutely need those 5 Virtual Servers, then you can add a weighting to your pricing to compensate for that.

So, let's say that your normal **Per User** rate for a Managed Support agreement is $100 per user per month, then that would mean a normal 10 seat client would come out at $1,000.

You can then add a 1.3 complexity multiplier for this **complex client**, which will then make the price for that client $130 per user per month or $1,300 overall.

You don't need to (and shouldn't) explain this to the prospect because you've told them that you're going to come up with Custom Bespoke pricing especially to suit them (remember, this is why you shouldn't display any pricing publicly anywhere).

From your position, you are offering the exact same offering that you're offering to a 10 seat client with only 1 server, but you're earning more from this **complex client** to cover the extra work you're going to have to do to patch, monitor and maintain the 4 x additional servers.

Obviously, another way to deal with **complex clients** if you have a lot of them is to split out your **Core Infrastructure** charge separate to your **Per User** pricing so that you can easily adjust and scale both of them separately.

PRO TIP: Here's something you can do if you come across a prospect who has a lot of **unnecessary** technology complexity in their business.

Perhaps they've had an Internal IT person who's had too much time on their hands and justified their own existence by building a complex network of virtual servers to keep themselves looking busy to the boss.

PRO TIP (Cont.): At its core, it's the clients' fault for letting their Internal IT person do what they did.

However, they have realized the error of their ways, sacked the idiot and engaged you to help simplify their complex craziness.

What you can do here is quote them a **Fixed Fee Project** (or perhaps multiple Fixed Fee Projects) to simplify and remove the **unnecessary complexity** from their network and bring them back to a normal baseline.

Then, for their **Monthly Support Agreement**, you can quote them what their normal monthly price would be <u>IF they were at your normal baseline</u> **AND** an **additional temporary** price that you charge to cover supporting the extra complexity until the simplification projects are finished.

It might look something like this on your Quotes, Agreements and Invoices:

		PRICING WITH TEMPORARY ADDITIONAL COMPLEXITY	Price	Total
☑	1	Core Infrastructure Management & Support	$1,500	$1,500
☑	1	Temporary Additional Complexity Management & Support	$850	$850

Doing this can give clients enough of a shove to put a priority on some important project work.

Then, once you've finished your initial Simplicity Project(s), you simply remove the Temporary Additional Complexity Fee from their invoice and bring their monthly costs down.

A win-win all round.

PART V

The Next Steps

JUST GET IT GOING

Having coached hundreds and hundreds of MSPs over the years, I've been in the unique position to see a lot of what's going on behind the scenes.

And one of the most common traits I've noticed in every single one of the most successful MSPs is that they **make quick decisions and they act fast.**

They do this, knowing full well that they **will make mistakes**, and the faster they make mistakes, the faster they can learn from them. Those learnings are what turns them into a **Best in Class MSP** far quicker than any of their peers.

On the flip side, the least successful MSPs I see, the ones working 60, 70 and 80+ hour weeks and earning barely anything, spend FAR too much time procrastinating on making decisions and trying to get things perfect.

Many years ago, one of my mentors and business coaches, Taki, saw me trying to get something absolutely perfect and whispered 5 simple words into my ear that have been bouncing around inside my head ever since and are forever etched into my memory.

He whispered... **"Done is better than perfect."**

This book is a perfect example.

I **could** have spent some extra time making it absolutely perfect.

But instead, I listened to Taki's words bouncing around in my head and got it **done** and into your hands as fast as I could, so that you can start learning the lessons from it and implementing the takeaways.

This was far more important to me than to hold back the information while I try to make the book perfect (unobtainable).

So, now whenever you're spending wasting time trying to get your Packages and Plans perfect, I want you to hear my voice (Aussie accent and all) bouncing around in your head screaming...

"Dude, done is better than perfect!"

YOUR NEXT STEPS

So, I want you to make a promise to me.

I want you to promise me that you won't spend any more than 10 hours over the next 30 days working on whatever the latest version of your Packages and Plans will be (based on what you've learned in this book), and then I want you to get them out in the marketplace.

There are oodles of businesses out there that **need you to rescue them** from their current bad (and probably dangerous) MSP.

So, get out there and **keep delivering awesome**. :-)

Thanks for reading and I wish you a bucket load of success for the future!

Nigel Moore

P.S. If you ever spot me at an industry event, conference, workshop or seminar (or maybe even out surfing), please come and say G'day. I **love** meeting fellow tech geeks from around this crazy planet of ours!

WHAT IS THE TECH TRIBE?

You've seen me make a few remarks about The Tech Tribe, and if you aren't already in our Tribe, then you might be wondering what the heck is this Tribal thing all about.

I hope that by laying out all that detail as much as I can, you'll now allow me to spend 57 seconds introducing you to our business.

Basically, in a 47-second nutshell, **The Tech Tribe** is a community of **Nimble MSPs** all around the world growing, learning, making mistakes and building their businesses together.

Our Tribe is headed up by our core group of Tribal Elders, including yours truly (Yep, me!) and other industry legends including Richard Tubb, James Stackhouse, Jamie Warner, Todd Kane, Andrew Moon and Craig Sharp (these guys are the cream of the crop when it comes to MSP industry knowledge).

When you join The Tech Tribe, you get access to loads of tools, resources and training to help you better run and grow your MSP.

In addition to all the juicy resources, training and templates, most importantly, you'll be joining a thriving, supportive and active community of hundreds of MSPs from all around the world. The beauty of this community is that it's not on Facebook or LinkedIn, so it's not full of trolls, bad advice and advertisements designed to pull you away from working ON your business.

We keep The Tech Tribe at a ridiculously low price point to make it accessible for all you **Nimble MSPs**. Because as I said before—I am a firm believer that you **Nimble MSPs** can really truly help change the world through Technology.

Because you've read this far, I've got a super-duper, steak-knife-readers-only special for joining our Tech Tribe. You can find more details at **https://thetechtribe.com/ profitbook.**

Hope to see you inside our Tribe one day!

Funnily enough, we actually don't do **Value-Based Pricing** for the **The Tech Tribe** because our mission to grow it into the world's leading community for MSPs, and to do that, we need to keep it at a super low price point.

We keep our Value-Based offerings for our higher-level intimate coaching programs; perhaps I'll see you in one of them one day.

SEND ME AN EMAIL!

I love hearing from readers, so feel free to shoot me an email to **nigel@thetechtribe.com** and say G'Day!

Or even better, let me know that you've used one of the strategies or tactics you've learned from within these pages (hopefully with great success)!

I promise to reply back, however fair warning, it might take me a few weeks as I'm one of those people that batches similar tasks together (like email replies about this book) so I can do them all in one go once or twice a month.

And, to be fair, let me set an expectation up front so there's no awkwardness between us. I'm in the business of advising, educating, mentoring and coaching, and it's one of the ways I feed my family. So, please don't ask for free help, advice or coaching via email as my PA will likely just direct you to one of my paid programs. AKA, I won't ask you for free IT help, don't ask me for free Business help. Cool? Rockin 😎

HELP ME OUT

Last, but not least—if you enjoyed reading this book and think it could help other Nimble MSPs, then I'd love, love, love if you could leave me a review on Amazon (5 stars of course, haha).

If you take a screenshot of your review and email it to me, I'll send you a little something special as a thank you gift!

ACKNOWLEDGEMENTS

Now, strap yourself in because this may sound a little corny and woo-woo. However, the first thing I want to show **incredible appreciation and gratitude** for are all the challenges, setbacks, bad days/weeks/months and years I've been hit with over the past two decades I've spent in the IT industry.

If I didn't have those bajillion troubles, dramas and problems to find solutions for over the years—I wouldn't be where I am today, and I wouldn't be able to help you MSPs in the way that I do.

A huge thank you to Richard Tubb and Karl Palachuk. I came across you two legends over a decade ago and started devouring everything you wrote. You were both my first unofficial mentors, and a lot of what I teach and coach has been inspired by you. I'm lucky enough now to count both of you as friends and business partners in crime. And if you're an MSP and you aren't following Richard and Karl, then put this book down now, and go Google them and follow them.

Thanks to the other industry veterans: Robert Crane, Gary Pica, Erick Simpson, Harry Brelsford and Robin Robins—I've also learned a lot from you all over the years, and for the lessons I've learned, I'm incredibly grateful. Thank you for what you do for the MSP industry.

Thank you to our Tribal Elders: Richard Tubb, Jim Stackhouse, Jamie Warner, Todd Kane, Andrew Moon and Craig Sharp—you rock stars are wizards in the MSP world, and I'm incredibly grateful to have you as part of our Tribe.

Thanks to our awesome bunch of Tech Tribers all around the world. There are hundreds and hundreds and hundreds of you now, and I'm inspired by the passion you have for making the world a better place through Technology. It's a true pleasure to be able to serve & support you.

Extra thanks to Tech Tribers: Scott Schulze, Chris Moroz, Simon Herzig, Kevin Sipma, Matt Pearce, Dan Baird, James Borg, Tom Fisher, Jeremy Johnson, Jon Dawkins, Leigh Wood, Tony Sollars, Clint Simonsen and David Szupnar for helping me improve this beast!

Thanks to Trish for giving me the kick up the backside to start my IT Business all those years ago. I wouldn't have created what I did if you hadn't helped me get the ball rolling.

Shout out to Rick, Rally & Fatima on Team Tribe for keeping the backend of our business running so I can focus on looking after our Tribe.

Thank you to Mike Capuzzi for being my Sherpa while climbing this book-writing mountain. I honestly wouldn't have done it without you.

Finally, this book and my journey wouldn't have happened without the support of my family.

Mum—for putting up with me for 40 revolutions around the sun, instilling a deep and empathetic work ethic in me and for being our babysitter on tap. Clem, for having to live with someone so deeply passionate and addicted to all things business and entrepreneurial (as much as I know you hate the word). And lastly, Harper-Read and Halliday—you crazy little humans are why I do what I do. Thank you—I appreciate your support more than I ever get across in words.

ABOUT NIGEL MOORE

NIGEL MOORE is a husband, dad, investor, speaker, entrepreneur and mentor to small businesses around the world (with a special focus on **Nimble MSPs**).

Instead of playing football with the cool kids in school, Nigel stayed at home and spent his afternoons and weekends typing code into his Commodore 64 from computer magazines, kicking off a lifelong fascination with all things Technology.

Nigel started officially earning money from the IT space in 1998 doing some consulting while he was studying an Information Science degree at university. This was quickly followed by a job at a local web development agency, where Nigel quickly rose to become the general manager (ultimately prompting him to follow his idol at the time, Bill Gates, to dropout of university).

In 2002, Nigel joined his first Outsourced IT Support firm, again becoming general manager a few years later. Then, in 2008, through a crazy turn of events, Nigel ended owning his own MSP (ask him about it if you ever meet him in person).

Nigel grew the MSP from a single person business to a small team over the next few years, and in 2014, Nigel, along with another friend, merged two MSPs together. They spent the next few years systemizing, hiring good people and working ON the combined business.

In 2016, they were given an offer they couldn't refuse, and the MSP was acquired.

In early 2017, Nigel founded The Tech Tribe, which is now fast becoming the world's leading community for MSPs, made up of hundreds of MSPs from around the world, all learning, growing and helping each other to better run and grow their businesses.

Nigel has a deep belief that everyone has their own special genius inside of them, and he loves helping small business owners work out how to find that genius and then spend as much time as possible working in it.

Nigel lives on the beach 90 minutes north of Sydney along with his wife, two daughters and their (loudly snoring) French Bulldog. He's a daily meditator & journaler, surfer, swimmer and snowboarder, and when he's not working or spending time with the family—you'll find him out riding waves in the ocean or dreaming about his next snowboarding trip.

For more details about The Tech Tribe, please visit **https://thetechtribe.com** or if you're interested in talking with Nigel about an **equity for advisory** arrangement or a **potential investment**, please send an email to **nigel@ teethcapital.com**.

READER BONUS

I recently spoke at a training event in London on **Packaging Your MSP Plans**, and it was recorded while being live streamed out to ~1,000 MSPs across Europe.

If you'd like to watch the video, simply head to the page below and click the **PLAY** button (don't worry, you don't have to opt in to watch the video).

It's around an hour and a great way to see some of the training included in this book from a different perspective and listen in as I answer some of the great questions asked by the audience.

packagepriceprofit.com/video

Made in the USA
Middletown, DE
09 May 2020